DATA
IMPACT

How legacy businesses
SAVE
LEVERAGE
ALIGN
SIMPLIFY
OPTIMIZE
GROW
to WIN

RITAVAN

R^ethink

First published in Great Britain in 2025
by Rethink Press (www.rethinkpress.com)

© Copyright Ritavan

Contents

Foreword

A s an avid reader and lifelong learner, I am honored to introduce this invaluable book that challenges conventional wisdom and offers a fresh perspective on data-driven business impact. Ritavan's experience, insight, and pragmatism shine through on every page, making this work an indispensable resource for business executives, entrepreneurs, and investors alike.

At the core of this transformative book lies the SLASOG Framework, a robust tool designed to navigate the complex landscape of data-driven decision-making:

- **Save:** Avoid costly groupthink mistakes and low-impact strategies

- **Leverage:** Identify and capitalize on your unique competitive advantages

- **Align:** Unify organizational efforts around clear, impactful goals

- **Simplify:** Reduce complexity to enhance adaptability and efficiency

- **Optimize:** Cultivate an empirically valid worldview for superior decision-making

- **Grow:** Focus on customer demand and embrace an abundance mindset

This framework is not mere theory – it represents battle-tested knowledge distilled from a decade of unwavering focus on data-driven impact. Ritavan's candid approach, devoid of hype and empty promises, is refreshingly pragmatic in an era of constant technological upheaval.

What distinguishes this book is its steadfast commitment to timeless principles rather than fleeting trends. Ritavan astutely observes that, while technology evolves at a breakneck pace, the fundamentals of business success remain relatively constant. By anchoring a strategy around these enduring elements, readers will be better equipped to thrive amidst uncertainty.

This book is more than just a collection of ideas – it is a resolute call to action. Ritavan challenges readers to think critically, act courageously, and obsess about impact. Through detailed case studies and practical worksheets, the book inspires us to immediately apply these concepts to real-world business scenarios.

As readers embark on this journey, they should heed the guiding principle: "Decisive opinions, adaptable stance." This book will push individuals to form well-reasoned opinions, test them rigorously, and adapt as new information emerges. It is this delicate balance of conviction and flexibility that separates truly successful leaders from the rest. I am confident that the insights within these pages will empower readers to navigate the complexities of our data-driven world and achieve remarkable results. So, roll up your sleeves, dive in, and prepare to transform your approach to business in the digital age.

Dr Marco Adelt
Insurtech entrepreneur and angel investor

Introduction

"Will the markets trade up or down?" asked the voice from the table to my right.

"I'm not really sure – I don't know the future," I shot back.

I had just graduated with a master's in mathematics and machine learning from France's elite École Normale Supérieure Paris-Saclay. I was still scarred from losing precious points in exams at the start of my master's – not because I wrote the wrong answer to a question or even the wrong proof, but because the structure of my proof wasn't drafted with requisite rigor.

"You get paid to have a view. It doesn't matter if you're wrong occasionally – just make sure you're right on average," my trading manager shot back at me.

I was in the first months of my first job, trading short-term physical power in the European energy markets. My manager was right. I couldn't hide behind the excuse of axiomatic rigor or the uncertainty of markets. I was getting paid to have a view and to act profitably on it.

Since then I have forced myself to always have a view on everything. Well, almost everything, but never statically or rigidly. Strong views, weakly held.

Technology forecaster Paul Saffo formulated this approach eloquently in 2008:

> "The fastest way to an effective forecast is often through a sequence of lousy forecasts. Instead of withholding judgment until an exhaustive search for data is complete, I will force myself to make a tentative forecast based on the information available, and then systematically tear it apart, using the insights gained to guide my search for further indicators and information. Iterate the process a few times, and it is surprising how quickly one can get to a useful forecast.

"Since the mid-1980s, my mantra for this process is 'strong opinions, weakly held.' Allow your intuition to guide you to a conclusion, no matter how imperfect – this is the 'strong opinion' part. Then – and this is the 'weakly held' part – prove yourself wrong. Engage in creative doubt. Look for information that doesn't fit, or indicators that pointing [sic] in an entirely different direction. Eventually your intuition will kick in, and a new hypothesis will emerge out of the rubble, ready to be ruthlessly torn apart once again. You will be surprised by how quickly the sequence of faulty forecasts will deliver you to a useful result."[1]

Clarity, courage, and impact

This is not just about having a view. It is about being right more often than not, especially by disagreeing with the consensus – being intelligently contrarian. That is where opportunities lurk and where big money is to be made; but how often do you have to be right to win big?

Tennis legend Roger Federer, in his commencement address to Dartmouth's 2024 graduating class, announced that he had won more than 80% of the 1,526 singles matches he played in his career.[2] No wonder he's considered one of the greatest tennis players of all time!

Federer then revealed that he won less than 54% of the points in those tennis matches. How does this 4% edge in winning points translate to winning over 80% of the games?

Winning a point depends on your relative edge over your opponent. If a match consisted of just one point, the probability of winning a game would be the same as winning a point. A slight increase in the probability of winning a single point gets leveraged and compounds over the four points that make up a game. In tennis, like in markets, even a small consistent edge can be leveraged to compound over time to deliver phenomenal results.

In 2012 Amazon founder and CEO Jeff Bezos, speaking to CTO Werner Vogels, said that he was frequently asked what would change in the following ten years, but never what would *not* change in that time.[3] Bezos claims that second question is actually the more important of the two, because you can build a business strategy around the things that are stable in time.

This book is not about a trendy new technology or a magical software tool or programming language that will solve all your problems. If you're looking for a silver bullet, then please put this book down and look elsewhere. I respect your time and don't want to disappoint you. The internet is full of the latest AI hype, and some of the smartest commercial talent in the world works in enterprise software sales. I'm sure a lot of vendors and consultants would love to take you out for dinner or play golf with you. I'm not selling you anything.

If you're looking for battle-tested knowledge and experience from a decade of obsessing about data-driven impact, then let's embark on this book together. Technology trends come and go, sometimes even before a commonly accepted term for a concept has been agreed on. Twenty years ago rules-based systems and linear regression were considered AI, then only neural networks and deep learning became AI, followed by only reinforcement learning being AI. Now, as I write this book, AI is synonymous only with large language models (LLMs). I will stay far away from the hornet's nest of commenting, influencing, selling, and fortune telling on the latest hyped technology trend that lasts for ever shorter periods.

The game of surfing the latest AI technology trend might be fun, but I haven't seen a magic fix yet, and I won't believe in one until I see it. Over the past decade a lot of reputed people have spoken about solving artificial general intelligence, raised hundreds of billions of dollars, and then ended up selling us advertising instead. We were promised self-driving cars in 2017, and in 2023 I was reluctantly forced to get my driver's license. We were promised companion robots for the elderly, and I still worry about my aging parents, who live halfway around the world. I'm tired of waiting for a knight in shining armor to come and take us into a brighter utopia. Even if that does happen, I'm sure we'll all have to pay a huge monthly subscription fee for the ride. No one ever consumed their way to glory.

What I have seen is that thinking rationally with an empirically valid worldview and solving foundational problems leads to phenomenal results. Both my work and that of others are presented in greater detail in the twelve case studies of this book. This book is for you if you are a business owner, executive, investor, or entrepreneur in a legacy industry, who wants to think from first principles about data-driven business impact. The book is based on principles and learnings that have helped me win at data-driven business impact over the past decade, which I have put into a framework that is designed to help you win over the next decade.

As an avid reader of books and listener of podcasts, I have relentlessly learned and leveraged the knowledge of countless operators, investors, leaders, authors, and thinkers. I have the privilege of standing on the shoulders of giants, and I readily and frequently cite their ideas and work through this book. If something piques your interest, I highly recommend you dig deeper by referring to the list of resources in the "Further Reading" section at the end of this book.

As an operator, I have deconstructed, synthesized, experimented, and applied the ideas of others to my work. Through this process, I have adapted, recombined, and reforged knowledge and experience into my framework, which has helped me get to my 80% match wins. It's about showing up, thinking clearly, acting courageously, and obsessing about impact. I want this to help you win at least 54% of the shots you play. Like in tennis or the markets, the rest should take care of itself.

Benchmark yourself first

The objective of this book is to create data-driven impact for you. It is impossible for you to measure that, though, unless we first benchmark where you stand now. Think of it like doing a blood test or ultrasound to assess your condition and help you with a diagnosis. Complete your SLASOG Scorecard here to get personalized results: www.slasog.com/scorecard

Introducing the SLASOG Framework

If you like things condensed and distilled because you are eager to act, then just read this section of front-loaded compact value. You can then read each chapter as and when you feel the need to. Your time is precious.

Act now because your longest lifetime-value customers are for the first time in human history a combination of nature, nurture, and data-driven algorithms.

Here is my SLASOG Framework for you:

1. Save

2. Leverage

3. Align

4. Simplify

5. Optimize

6. Grow

1. Save: Avoid costly groupthink mistakes and low-impact strategies

- You can save money by avoiding *spray-and-pray*, low-impact antipatterns with high failure rates.

- You can save money by avoiding boiling-the-ocean-style, wicked problems with unclear, impactless, and unquantifiable objectives and solutions.

- The wisdom of crowds is valid only under certain conditions; you can't crowdsource a winning strategy.

- Groupthink – packaged as *best practices* – is the most dangerous type of poison because it is the most politically convenient.

- Good decision-making comes not just from mental clarity but also from behavioral and emotional awareness.

2. Leverage: Identify and capitalize on your unique competitive advantages

- Understand the power laws in your customer demand and data.

- Think how you can leverage the unique legacy assets of your business.

- Recognize your unfair non-digital advantage and how you can leverage it.

- Establish how you can use counter-positioning as leverage to grow your new data-driven business.

- Determine how you can productize the leveraged impact you deliver to your customers.

3. Align: Unify organizational efforts around clear, impactful goals

- Ascertain your North Star metric and whether your entire organization is aligned to it.

- Establish a centralized fast-approval leadership structure, with decentralized execution and accountability.

- Use *commander's intent* to empower your teams to execute autonomously and with full alignment by ensuring clear communication.

- Employ *metrics that matter* to empower your teams while also aligning them to your North Star metric.

- Ensure your teams are incentivized and evaluated on high-leverage impact and outcomes instead of easier-to-measure activity.

4. Simplify: Reduce complexity to enhance adaptability and efficiency

- Simplify products to stay well above the nuisance threshold of users and build good habits.

- Increase adaptability by abandoning blueprint-based, committee-consensus decision-making in true uncertainty.

- Identify overhead tasks and processes you can completely discard, combine, modularize, or automate.

- Radically rethink processes through simplification and redesign by refactoring past incremental fixes, thereby increasing antifragility.

- Modularize complexity to standardize, simplify, and ensure adaptability, while scaling to avoid collapse from the growing costs of complexity.

5. Optimize: Cultivate an empirically valid worldview for superior decision-making

- Know the type of environment you operate in to design and improve your decision-making and learning approach.

- Identify all empirically valid abstractions that are mathematically optimizable for the environment you operate in.

- Extract maximum regularity from your environment to minimize randomization in decision-making.

- Identify irreducible uncertainties of the environment that you should embrace to prevent oversimplification.

- Optimize the impact of your decisions by taking the full distribution of outcomes into account.

6. Grow: Focus on customer demand and embrace an abundance mindset

- Shift from a scarcity mindset, focused on resource constraints, to an abundance mindset. Achieve this by prioritizing customer demand and unmet needs, and leveraging data-driven technologies, to deliver 10× better outcomes.

- Look beyond your existing supply and unlock abundant demand to drive growth through targeted investments and partnerships.

- Compound growth by building your data-driven progressive impact funnel and long-term optimized flywheel.

- Solve for infrequent products by building a portfolio of higher-frequency value, delivering data-driven products, content, and assets.

- Leverage your legacy assets, align everything to a North Star metric, simplify the rest, and optimize by accelerating value delivery. To grow, iterate this with asymmetric bets, and focus on word-of-mouth recommendations.

ONE
Save

In this first chapter of the SLASOG Framework, we'll look at how you can save money by avoiding anti-patterns, wicked problems, groupthink mistakes, and low-cost strategies.

Start by saving money

Everyone is probably telling you to start spending money to become a digital data-driven business. I want you to first save money. This will provide you with savings to use as seed capital for the rest of the principles presented in this book.

A lot of so-called best practices and conventional wisdom are ineffective groupthink that is expensive, with little – or often no – value created for you. Digital transformation is the trendy thing that every vendor will ask you to embark on. Organizational changes and transformations are generally very hard, but digital transformation initiatives seem to have significantly worse failure rates. A study of more than 1,000 companies by consulting firm Bain & Company found that the success rate of conventional organizational transformations was 12%, while that of digital transformations was only 5%.[4]

In their meta-study "Covid-19 has accelerated digital transformation, but may have made it harder not easier," Professor Michael Wade and his co-author Jialu Shan, from IMD Business School, identify eleven studies that empirically evaluate the success or failure of digital transformations.[5] Several of these studies were conducted on hundreds of companies and arrived at different failure rates, ranging from about 80% to about 97%. Based on this, they arrive at 87.5% aggregate failure rate. The conclusion is that only about one in eight digital transformation initiatives is considered a success by the very people involved.

The most fun way to find this out for yourself is to get vendor or consultant friends drunk and hear them complain about the meaninglessness of soviet-style multi-year company-wide digital transformation.

Stop using the spray and pray approach

One common approach to digital transformation is defining use cases, either by trusting supposed best practices recommended by vendors, or by crowdsourcing ideas from people in your company. These use cases are by design narrow and disconnected. If they are recommended by the vendor, they are narrow and disconnected because the integration and personalization costs, as well as the accountability for the vendor, are minimized. If they are crowdsourced, the use cases are narrow and disconnected because no single person or function in your company has simultaneously the width and depth required to formulate a coherent value maximizing strategy. In any case, if you rank and prioritize use cases by committee or consensus, to keep the budget under control you will prefer those that are narrowly defined. Also, to spread your bets to make it look safe, you will probably prioritize independent narrow use cases. I call this *spray and pray* – hedging your bets by opting for unexceptional, supposedly risk-free portfolios of solutions.

Spray and pray is an antipattern that should be avoided. An antipattern is a common response to a recurring problem that, despite initially appearing to be an appropriate and effective response to a problem, has more bad consequences than good ones. It is usually ineffective and risks being highly counterproductive. Start by saving the money you are or were planning to spend on spray and pray. After reading this book, you'll be able to use that money to successfully drive data-driven impact.

Narrow use cases are like guerilla attacks – they're great if you're losing and want to desperately defend territory against a stronger foe, but as a large incumbent, they're not how you conquer new lands and win on the offensive. If you deconstruct your worst digital experiences as a customer, you'll notice that the business behind them is probably doing some form of spray and pray.

Reasons to avoid spray and pray

One of the reasons spray and pray fails miserably is because it is based on industrial paradigm thinking, which relies on incrementalism and predictable outcomes. In the digital and data-driven paradigm, problems cannot be decomposed into small incremental steps, because problems are not predictable, and they change with the data.

Another reason spray and pray does not work is because it is at the center of a direct conflict of objectives between the core business and new initiatives. If you are concurrently optimizing for developing something new, and minimizing the risk that it affects something that already exists, then – on a scale of one to ten – the consensus decision will be to pick a seven – politically the most comfortable choice. This doesn't maximize the success of the outcome, though. Sarah Travel initially said that sevens kill companies in the context of hiring and talent management, and Matt Lerner applied this to the prioritization of growth initiatives.[6] This is another reason why spray and pray fails.

Wisdom of crowds?

The wisdom of the crowds is commonly used to justify crowdsourced decisions. The underlying idea is that the aggregate decisions of large groups of people should be better than any one individual. The Condorcet jury theorem provides a simple mathematical framework to model when this assumption fails.[7]

Wisdom of crowds, and deliberative consensus-based decision-making for building something that is in direct conflict with the objectives of the core business, structurally results in sevens being chosen. This is a disaster for you.

Let's say you have crowdsourced a long list of twenty to fifty use cases across your company. Next you set up a committee to vote on which use cases should be allocated budgets. You start by gathering yes and no votes for one use case at a time, and a majority decision is required to allocate a budget to that use case. If each voter makes an independent decision, and the probability of each voter making the correct decision in each case is strictly greater than 50%, then Condorcet's jury theorem proves that having more people on the committee increases the overall probability of a correct group decision. Otherwise, it is guaranteed that the committee will reach the wrong decision. Are you sure, though, that every single person on your committee is making an independent decision that is at least 50% correct every time?

The independence of decision-making of each member of a committee is a far shot. I have never seen every member of any committee make independent decisions, because of the consensus-enforcing structure of the committee itself. Other common biases that occur are:

- A lack of diversity in perspectives

- Individual lack of expertise for a given topic

- Unequal availability of or access to information

Consensus also might work well for yes or no decisions, but it fails with more complex, multidimensional outcomes. Committees are great for politically comfortable decisions but rarely lead to successful ones.

Stop boiling the ocean

Aspiring to be personally at the bleeding edge of technology is the tech equivalent of fast fashion. It has short lifecycles, it is expensive, and it results in a lot of wasted resources. Doing this for your business is expensive, unreliable, and – most importantly – does not automatically result in any value creation. Digital for the sake of digital is tech consumerism. It makes the vendors producing the tech richer, and it turns you into a constantly high-spending consumer. This is what I call *boiling the ocean* – it can never work.

Technology tools are evolving at a faster pace than ever. Software and AI tooling are best developed and optimized with the user in the loop, so if you're always an early adopter of technology, you're essentially signing up for the software equivalent of medical clinical trials. If you find it exhilarating to try out the latest tech toys, then feel free to indulge in that hobby, but do yourself a favor and keep it as a hobby.

Warren Buffett's long-time business partner, the late Charlie Munger, had a telling anecdote that illustrates how the best investors and operators understand how tech consumerism does not lead to any value creation for the buyer of the new technology. Munger explained how, while they were working in the textile industry, Buffett was told about a newly invented loom that could potentially double their production levels. Buffett's response was that he would then have to exit the textile business. His reasoning was that the benefits of the increase in production would go to the buyer of the finished textiles and to the seller of the new loom, not to the company that bought the new equipment.[8]

Digital transformation by boiling the ocean is a wicked problem. *Wicked* in this context does not mean evil – it means impossible to solve. The definition of wicked problems is credited to Horst Rittel, who was a professor of decision theory in Germany.[9]

Wicked problems have the following characteristics, as defined by Jeff Conklin:

- They cannot be understood until their solutions have been found.

- They have no stopping rule, ie they can never be seen as completely solved.

- Solutions to wicked problems are neither right nor wrong, and the solutions can be attempted only once.

- Each wicked problem is unique, requiring a novel solution, with no alternative solutions.[10]

Doesn't that sound like the boiling-the-ocean digital transformation that vendors and consultants are pitching to you?

Obsessing about the customer is hard. It is much easier to hide behind a frenzy of activities like moving to the cloud, upgrading to a new CRM, migrating to another ERP version, or buying the trendiest "AI" SaaS solution. There is an army of consultants waiting to indulge this urge and make you feel good.

Your customer does not care what technology you use or how you run your business. Success comes from creating value and delivering impact to delight the customer. The only thing your customer cares about is how you delight them. That is the one and only North Star that matters to you and your business. If you want to create value for your business, you need to stop thinking like a consumer and start thinking like a producer. Like most things in life, the real value in technology is not in consuming it; it is in leveraging technology to create value for your customers.

The company that created the cloud computing market – and continues to dominate it two decades later – is not a consumer of technology. It is a producer of technology, it is obsessed with the customer, and it works backward from the customer. For a case study on how Amazon's customer obsession drove its growth, check the end of this chapter.

Groupthink packaged as best practices

Charlie Munger famously said, "Show me the incentive and I will show you the outcome."[11] Given the structural misalignment of incentives between your objectives and those of vendors and consultants, it is not surprising that the outcomes can be disastrous across the board.

Differing approaches to digital transformation

When you search for digital transformation, you see a lot of pages and content produced by vendors and consultants. Software vendors generally define digital transformation as the process of embedding technology (obviously their software) into every area of your business. Alternatively, they offer digital infrastructure then move your entire business onto their infrastructure. The objective of the vendor is to sell you their solution. If they offer infrastructure or a platform, they want you to migrate your entire business to those. Otherwise, they want you to put their product as a patch on some small part of your business. Usually, the vendor tries to make the process as minimally invasive as possible so that they have fewer customization and integration costs. This approach can be useful for covering painful steps, or for limited incremental improvements, but it is far from transformative.

Consultants define digital transformation as follows:

- It involves multiyear, long-term journeys rather than one-time projects.

- It is about constantly deploying technology at scale to create value, while blending human and technical capabilities.

- It is about changing culture and steadily building human and cultural capacity.

To make digital transformation sound less grand and more approachable, consultants often throw in a small AI use case as bait so that you can get started right away without a massive budget. Unlike the vendors that tend to be minimally invasive, consultants are consummate surgeons who want to cut open your entire business. It is always more lucrative to have a larger scope, and if things go wrong, it is easier to list the vast quantity of activities done or protocols followed without being pinned down for accountability. This approach, with its vast scope and lack of accountability, is structurally more transformative for the consultant than it is for you.

Both vendors and consultants want to close a sale. They market their solutions as low-risk because they are very narrowly scoped, minimally invasive, and barely incremental. In both cases, the objective is to derisk the sale by defining a very narrow or a very large scope to avoid accountability. The incentive is the sale.

The consequences of groupthink

Lack of accountability, combined with the smokescreen of respectability and status, leads to the worst kind of groupthink. This is the kind of groupthink that can continue unchallenged at scale, despite repeated losses, failures, and disasters.

An interesting historical example of this phenomenon is Napoleon's success against his opponents on the battlefield. According to one source, he fought about sixty battles in total and lost only seven – an 88% success rate. Including naval battles and his campaigns in Egypt and Russia is probably not relevant, as he mainly fought land battles in Europe. To what extent did Napoleon's success rate in battle depend on his adversaries being unable to adapt to his first principles approach?

Considering his most significant battles, Napoleon's success rate against the Austrians, Prussians, and Russians is well above 70%, since Blücher was late to Waterloo, and the Russian victory was at best pyrrhic. With success rates this high, Napoleon's boast "I have destroyed the Austrian army by simply marching" sounds rather factual.[12] His adversaries were always significantly older than him and, due to their family lineage or status, were not held accountable or sidelined, despite their repeated incompetence and defeats.

Unlike his adversaries, Napoleon meticulously prepared for each battle with a first principles approach – by gathering intel, choosing the battlefield, and understanding the enemy commanders. Wellington was interestingly about the same age as Napoleon and studied his tactics in great detail to develop his own first principles strategy before Waterloo.

Spray and pray and boiling the ocean – so-called best practices – have emerged through a lack of understanding of the core principles of value creation in the industrial, digital, and data-driven paradigms. They have grown through misaligned incentives and groupthink and have resulted in shockingly high failure rates, wasted resources, and a lack of trust that has impeded productivity gains and growth.

That is why, in this book, we go back to the drawing board to think things through from first principles. First principles thinking is the practice of questioning every assumption you think you know about a given problem and then creating a new solution from scratch. It is one of the best ways to:

- Break out of routine failures
- Think critically for yourself

- Unleash your analytical and creative capabilities
- Move from incremental linear results to tremendous non-linear outcomes

Behavioral and emotional antipatterns

Billionaire operator and investor Brad Jacobs speaks about the power of *thought experiments*, or *Gedankenexperimenten*.[13] This is something Einstein regularly did to reduce complex relationships in physics to easily imaginable scenarios. Brad Jacobs uses thought experiments as a strategic tool to equip him with unique perspectives by challenging conventional wisdom, asking *What if* questions, generating worst-case outcomes, simulating future investments, etc.

Doing this is cheaper than cloud computing. You simply need to sit back and think calmly, unleashing your analytical rigor and unfettered creativity, to evoke future trends, plan scenarios, explore possibilities, identify risks, and find hidden opportunities.

Trusting our instincts

When faced with uncertainty, we typically fall back on some primordial instincts. Unlike the rest of this book, the observations here are not based on empirical research, historical case studies, or the ideas of seminal thinkers or trends. These ideas are primarily based on personal observations of my own

Gedankenexperimenten, as well as those of others I have worked with, and loosely inspired by research and frameworks from behavioral psychology, evolutionary biology, and entrepreneurship.

This section is about recognizing that our decisions and actions are not entirely rational. Along with good reasoning and arguments, there is also an equally important emotional component that drives our decisions and actions, and their consequences. That is why deconstructing mental models with rational arguments is necessary, but doing so is not a sufficient criterion to drive change.

Just as I went to the foundations of our minds, history, and evolution to deconstruct the problems with conventional wisdom and approaches, I want to go now to the fundamental source of our emotions. The nuanced and sophisticated emotions we feel are hard to describe, quantify, and measure, but the fundamental evolutionary mechanisms that drive them are easier to frame. The reason for this is that these basal responses are triggered at such a deep, evolutionarily hardcoded level, that they have come to define our species' existence and current state.

The reptile

We all have that gut-wrenching response when faced with perceived danger. That is what I call the reptile, the involuntary unconscious evolutionary reflex – often simply when we encounter something new or unknown. We all have the reptile, and it is critical we do not dismiss or ignore it, as it causes a lot of harm if it is not given requisite care and attention.

The reptile's repertoire is made up of freeze, flight, fight, and fawn. The common thread that unites these various reactions – the origin of its reflexes – is fear. In the context of this book, the reptile freezes, ignoring and avoiding change. It stops thinking and acting, and it delays decisions and actions. The other response of the reptile is flight from accountability and responsibility, often manifested in multiyear digital transformation initiatives with poor ROIC and impractically lengthy payback periods. Acting out of fear, the reptile tries to fight through incremental defensive steps, which result in narrowly scoped use cases that are supposed to reduce risk but end up in greater failure rates. Finally, with all other fear responses exhausted, the reptile chooses to fawn by blindly copying mainstream conventional wisdom and getting hijacked by vendors. It's fascinating how groupthink and conventional wisdom is born and amplified from fear-based responses.

The monkey

Now that we have characterized the modus operandi of the reptile, who is the monkey?

I define the monkey as the next iteration of fear – basically a more emotionally sophisticated and energized version of the reptile. The reptile is the first basal instinctive response to fear – raw, without filters – with its origins in evolutionary survival. The monkey is the next stage, with less survival angst but more intense emotions and energy. The monkey's responses cannot be categorized into simple reflexes of freeze, flight, fight, and fawn, but its modus operandi results in similar outcomes.

The monkey is emotionally reactive and is not bothered with deep understanding and strategy. It wants to jump into action and be seen to be doing things. It's the overenthusiastic personality that gets excited but lacks the rigor and discipline to think things through from first principles before taking the plunge. Just as with the reptile, overlooking or shunning the monkey results in disastrous consequences. It is important to acknowledge the monkey yet try to iterate to the next level.

The monkey also craves novelty and excitement, jumping from one shiny trend and buzzword to the next, without really understanding or caring for impact or value creation. The monkey has whipped up, surfed, and crashed on the many hype waves we have seen over the past decades, from deep learning to reinforcement learning to LLMs, until the next new exciting buzzword becomes a trend. Given this continuous superficial distraction, the monkey is neither concerned about nor capable of value creation.

Given its passion for novelty and excitement, the monkey is distracted and impulsive, never trying to understand the big picture or develop a worldview. Its lack of interest in clarity and rigorous thinking results in a lack of vision and purpose. Along with this, the monkey is a sucker for instant, short-term gratification. Given its other traits, it has no capability of understanding and hence wants fast, predictable rewards. The monkey's obsession with instant gratification leads it to see value only in incrementalism and small steps, even though those lead nowhere in the long term. Finally, because the monkey is fundamentally lost but emotionally intense, it craves social validation and approval, looking for comfort in crowds, trends, groupthink, and common practices.

In their book *AI Snake Oil*, scientists Arvind Narayanan and Sayash Kapoor argue that broken institutions are the ones most susceptible to AI snake oil, ie spurious AI quick fixes.[14] Time and again, history has shown that the mirage of technology was misused to activate the reptile or monkey in the minds of executives and investors. Of course, there is no repository for all the failed initiatives and disastrous investments made by companies. However, from the self-reported 80–90% failure rate of digital transformation initiatives, it is easy to estimate how widespread the problem is. This is why understanding the emotional foundation of decisions is critical to success – making sure that the reptile or monkey is not allowed to get out of control.

DISCUSSION POINT: Save money now by avoiding antipatterns and wicked problems

Discuss these five points with your team and start saving money right away:

1. Money can be saved by avoiding spray-and-pray, low-impact antipatterns with high failure rates.

2. Money can be saved by avoiding boiling-the-ocean-style, wicked problems with unclear, impactless, and unquantifiable objectives.

3. The wisdom of crowds is valid only under certain conditions, and you can't crowdsource a winning strategy.

4. Groupthink packaged as best practices is the most dangerous type of snake oil because it is the most politically convenient.

5. Good decision-making comes not just from mental clarity but also from behavioral and emotional awareness.

Customer-obsessed giants

The following two case studies illustrate how customer-obsessed businesses founded around the turn of the millennium successfully evolved from their legacy physical origins to become technology pioneers. They achieved this by:

- Obsessing about customers

- Building technology instead of consuming technology

- Avoiding antipatterns and wicked problems

CASE STUDY: Revolutionizing technology – How Jeff Bezos took Amazon from selling books to dominating the cloud computing market

Jeff Bezos, founder and almost three-decade-long CEO of Amazon, took the company from its position as an online bookseller to that of a global leader in e-commerce, and to creating and dominating the cloud computing market. Central to this epic evolution was his relentless focus on customer needs, an iterative flywheel strategy, and a willingness to be misunderstood for long periods while pioneering groundbreaking innovations like Amazon Web Services (AWS).

Summary

Amazon's journey of development epitomizes the power of customer obsession and disciplined productization. By focusing on long-term value creation and leveraging its internal technological expertise, Amazon launched AWS in 2006, which became the backbone of the digital economy. This case study delves into how Bezos's principles, including insights from his shareholder letters, has guided Amazon's extraordinary diversification and growth over almost three decades.

Context

Amazon was founded in 1994 as an online bookstore, operating with the mission to become "Earth's most customer-centric company." By the early 2000s

Amazon had already disrupted traditional retail with its customer-obsessed approach and operational efficiency.

While scaling its e-commerce operations, Amazon encountered technology challenges like providing easy-to-use storage computing infrastructure for development to its affiliate partners and internal engineering teams. These challenges laid the foundation for AWS, launched in 2006 as a suite of on-demand cloud computing services. AWS enabled easy, cheap, and fast access to scalable computing power, enabling startups and enterprises alike to build new applications without investing in costly infrastructure upfront but instead by renting it from AWS.

Challenges

- **Complexity of e-commerce:** Delighting millions of customers required scalable and reliable infrastructure, which traditional IT solutions couldn't deliver efficiently at the time.

- **Capital-intensive growth:** Expanding Amazon's core business necessitated significant investment. This prompted Bezos to explore new revenue streams that leveraged the company's unique capabilities and unfair advantage, and which aligned with its customer-centric mission.

- **Misunderstanding and skepticism:** When AWS launched, many doubted that a retail company could succeed in a highly technical and enterprise-focused industry. Countless investment analysts wrote memos questioning Bezos's decision.

- **Category creation:** Convincing businesses to migrate to cloud computing involved overcoming entrenched reliance on traditional on-premise IT infrastructure and staff.

Methodology

Bezos guided Amazon's evolution using foundational principles detailed in his annual shareholder letters: customer obsession, long-term thinking, and operational excellence.

1. **Customer-centric innovation:** Bezos is obsessed with solving customer pain points – for example, consumers through e-commerce, or software developers through AWS. AWS addressed the need for affordable, scalable, and reliable IT solutions that were underserved when AWS was first launched.

2. **Spinning the flywheel:** Amazon's flywheel strategy connected customer satisfaction, operational efficiency, and reinvestment. AWS became a natural extension of this model, leveraging internal expertise to create a new revenue stream through the productization of existing tech assets.

3. **Willingness to be misunderstood:** Bezos championed the idea of pursuing ideas others might not even understand for long periods. AWS faced skepticism but was built on a long-term vision of transforming IT services. Bezos explicitly wrote in his shareholder letters that he was willing to be misunderstood for a long period. The ability to be an intelligent maverick is a huge moat in a business world plagued by groupthink.

4. **Iterative, rapid experimentation:** Amazon's culture of "high-velocity decision-making" and willingness to experiment allowed AWS to grow quickly in response to customer needs and feedback.

5. **Scalable technology development:** Amazon standardized its internal systems into modular components and robust APIs, enabling the creation

of reusable tools like S3 for storage and EC2 for computing. These became cornerstones of AWS's product strategy.

6. **Building an ecosystem:** AWS empowered developers, startups, and enterprises with tools to build fast, efficiently, and conveniently. This ecosystem drove adoption and created a virtuous cycle of network-based recommendation and growth.

Outcomes

- **Explosive growth:** AWS became the fastest-growing segment of Amazon, reaching over USD 100 billion in annual revenue by 2025 and commanding a leading position in the global cloud market.

- **Technological leadership:** AWS introduced industry-defining products like Lambda (serverless computing) and S3 (simple storage service), becoming a pioneer and market leader and setting benchmarks for the cloud industry.

- **Diversified revenue streams:** AWS provided high-margin, essentially recession-proof revenue, insulating Amazon from the cyclical pressures of retail, and funding further investment in new products.

- **Global impact:** AWS powers some of the world's largest companies, startups, and governments, becoming indispensable infrastructure for the digital economy globally.

- **Legendary culture:** Bezos's principles, articulated in his shareholder letters and leadership principles, became guiding tenets for ambitious customer-centric organizations worldwide.

Key takeaways

1. **Customer obsession drives technology:** By focusing on solving customer problems, Amazon identified new opportunities and built solutions like AWS that created massive customer and then shareholder value.

2. **Think long-term:** Bezos's willingness to invest in initiatives that took years to mature demonstrated the importance of patience and resilience in achieving breakthrough success, with a rigorous culture of ownership and fast decision-making.

3. **Leverage unique assets and expertise:** AWS emerged from Amazon's internal challenges, proving the potential of repurposing internal capabilities to address external markets and generate new revenue streams with high margins.

4. **Adapt and scale:** Amazon's iterative approach to building AWS ensured it could respond quickly to emerging or unmet customer needs and scale to meet demand to grow.

Conclusion

Jeff Bezos's epic growth of Amazon, from an online retailer to a global leader in cloud computing, exemplifies the power of long-term leveraged bets, aligned customer obsession, and optimized operational excellence. By addressing internal challenges to create solutions that resonated with new groups of customers, AWS became a cornerstone of Amazon's success.

Bezos's principles offer a roadmap for businesses seeking to innovate, scale, and redefine their industries through relentless customer obsession, building technology instead of consuming it, and avoiding antipatterns and wicked problems.

CASE STUDY: Revolutionizing entertainment – How Reed Hastings took Netflix from DVD rentals to streaming

Reed Hastings, cofounder and former CEO of Netflix, grew the company from a DVD rental service to a global streaming powerhouse by obsessing over customer needs. His relentless focus on delivering convenience, personalized experiences, and seamless technology revolutionized how the world consumes entertainment.

Summary

Netflix's journey, from mailing DVDs by post to becoming the leader in streaming entertainment, demonstrates the power of putting customers at the heart of every technology decision. By prioritizing convenience, personalization, and original content, Hastings created a business model that scaled globally and reshaped an entire legacy industry dominated by traditional incumbents. Netflix's story provides lessons in customer obsession, relentless adaptation, and long-term disruptive vision.

Context

Netflix was founded in 1997 by Reed Hastings and Marc Randolph as a DVD rental-by-mail service. The business gained initial traction by offering flat monthly subscriptions and eliminating late fees, setting itself apart from competitors like Blockbuster. Netflix catered to movie aficionados interested in older classics, thereby delighting a customer group that was underserved by its much larger rival, Blockbuster, which focused on the latest blockbuster releases.

By the mid-2000s advancements in broadband technology and shifting consumer habits presented a new opportunity: streaming. Hastings recognized that to stay ahead, Netflix needed to evolve beyond DVDs. This shift would involve massive investments in technology, content licensing, and eventually original productions, all while staying true to the company's mission of delighting customers with the best entertainment.

Challenges

- **Shifting technology paradigm**
  - Transitioning from DVDs to streaming required building robust streaming technology and infrastructure from scratch.
  - Licensing digital rights for popular movies and TV shows was complex and very expensive.

- **Content ownership and growth**
  - Maintaining customer loyalty while transitioning to a new platform posed risks, especially as the DVD business declined.
  - Reliance on licensed content created vulnerabilities as studios launched competing platforms and reclaimed their rights.

Methodology

1. **Customer-first approach**
   - Hastings believed in obsessing over customer needs, making customer satisfaction the key to long-term growth.

- Netflix invested heavily in algorithms to personalize recommendations, ensuring each user received a personalized viewing experience.

2. **Investing in streaming technology**
   - Netflix pioneered adaptive streaming technology, ensuring high-quality video across devices and internet speeds.
   - Netflix built a user-friendly and seamless experience on its streaming platform.

3. **Building a content empire**
   - Recognizing the limitations of licensed content, Hastings began producing original programming in 2013, starting with *House of Cards*.
   - By owning its intellectual property, Netflix gained control over its content library, reducing dependency on external studios.

4. **Data-driven decision-making**
   - Netflix leveraged proprietary viewing data to guide decisions about content acquisition, production, and user interface design.
   - Insights from analyzing proprietary data enabled Netflix to create and market hits like *Stranger Things* and *The Crown* by developing a granular understanding of genres, epochs, and character types that lead people to binge-watch on the platform, maximizing viewer engagement.

5. **Global expansion**
   - Hastings championed a scalable model, launching Netflix in over 190 countries and investing in local content to appeal to diverse audiences.

- The recommendation algorithm developed by Netflix personalizes diverse content to user preferences.

Outcomes

- **Explosive growth**
  - Netflix grew from about 1 million subscribers in 2003 to over 282 million by 2025.
  - Revenue surged from USD 272 million in 2003 to over USD 33 billion in 2025.

- **Industry leadership**
  - Netflix became synonymous with streaming, thereby differentiating its brand and reputation, and outpacing competitors in market share and innovation.
  - Original programming earned critical acclaim, with Netflix securing multiple Academy Awards and Emmys over the years.

- **Global customer loyalty**
  - Personalized recommendations and a diverse content library kept churn rates low, cementing Netflix as a household name.
  - Netflix's expansion into international markets brought series like *Money Heist* and *Squid Game* to global audiences, redefining entertainment's cultural reach and diversity of content.

Key takeaways

1. **Customer obsession wins**
   - Hastings' focus on solving customer pain points – such as eliminating late fees or creating personalized experiences – was central to Netflix's success.

- By pivoting to streaming before it became mainstream, Netflix stayed ahead of the curve and disrupted itself rather than waiting for competitors to do so.

2. **Building leveraged tech and IP assets**
   - Netflix's commitment to building user-friendly streaming technology laid the foundation for a seamless, scalable platform.
   - Original programming and investment in IP assets allowed Netflix to own its content and differentiate itself from competitors reliant on licensing deals.

Conclusion

Reed Hastings' deliberate and multiyear evolution of Netflix, from a DVD rental service to a streaming giant, exemplifies the power of customer-obsessed technology development and bold leadership. By focusing on what customers wanted – convenience, personalization, and quality – Netflix became a category leader in digital entertainment.

Hastings' legacy provides a masterclass on how businesses can anticipate change and invest in developing category-defining technology to scale globally and create lasting value, instead of wasting resources on spray and pray or boiling-the-ocean digital transformation disasters.

TWO

Leverage

Think from first principles how you can leverage your assets – your unfair non-digital advantage to grow your data-driven business. Thinking from first principles will give you an edge over people who follow set templates or recipes. This chapter will clarify the strategy and execution that will allow you to identify and capitalize on your unique competitive advantages.

Sevens kill companies: Satisficing

Leverage is about achieving maximum impact with minimum input. Find your leverage and use it. If no one finds your leverage bold or risky, then it cannot be a high-leverage decision. Something high-leverage has to have clear directionality and cannot be arrived at by consensus. When you map your options on a scale from 1 to 10, everyone complains about how workplace politics kills high-leverage decisions and instead picks politically comfortable sevens. This affects all kinds of critical decisions, including hiring decisions, investment decisions, and growth decisions. Eventually, by repeatedly picking politically comfortable sevens over long periods, businesses guarantee their decline.

Is there an evolutionary behavioral reason for this irrational decision?

Why do people pick sevens by consensus?

Probability matching

Let's do a thought experiment. Suppose we played a game where I toss a coin, and you guess heads or tails. If you guess correctly, I pay you one dollar, and if you guess wrongly, you pay me one dollar. After a few tosses, you notice that the relative frequency of heads is about 70%. The rational decision for you now is to call heads on every toss, as it maximizes your cumulative expected payoff. However, across studies, the vast majority of subjects don't pick the strategy with the highest expected payoff. Instead, they do what is called *probability matching*. In the example above, they would pick heads about 70% of the time, and tails for about 30% of the time.

There is an interesting high-stakes historical example of this behavior. Nobel Laureate Daniel Kahneman's long-time research collaborator, Amos Tversky, shared the example below with financial economist Stephen Ross, famous for arbitrage pricing theory and the Cox-Ross-Rubinstein option pricing model. Ross in turn shared it with finance professor Andrew Lo, of adaptive market hypothesis fame. Unfortunately, they were not able to confirm the details with Tversky before his untimely passing, but the example gives a fascinating illustration of probability matching.[15]

During World War II, pilots and crew members in the US Air Force faced a critical decision before each bombing mission over Germany: whether to wear a parachute or a flak jacket. At the time, parachutes were bulky; and flak jackets were even bulkier, as they contained steel plates for protection (long before the invention of Kevlar). The bulkiness made it impractical to wear both simultaneously, forcing the crew to choose one.

Parachutes were essential for survival if the bomber was shot down by German anti-aircraft artillery, while flak jackets protected against shrapnel from high-explosive shells that often penetrated the plane's fuselage. Statistically, the likelihood of being hit by anti-aircraft fire was significantly higher than the risk of the aircraft being shot down. Additionally, each mission's risks were independent of previous ones, meaning there was no cumulative advantage or changing odds.

Rationally, the optimal choice would have been to wear flak jackets consistently. However, bomber crews often alternated between wearing parachutes and flak jackets, roughly matching their choices to the relative probabilities of being shot down versus being hit by anti-aircraft fire. This probability-matching behavior puzzled and frustrated military officials, who tried unsuccessfully to persuade crews to prioritize flak jackets to enhance their safety.

This kind of probability-matching behavior has been observed among other species – including goldfish, pigeons, monkeys, and even ants – so there might be an evolutionary reason for this seemingly irrational behavior. The evolutionary explanation is that unpredictable environments, coupled with the following factors, led species to adopt a probability-matching approach:

- Intractable wicked problems

- Trade-off between low-effort good enough and high-effort optimal outcome

- Efficiency of computing and energy

This approach – making decisions that meet the minimum criteria for success without picking the best outcome – is called *satisficing*. The term – a combination of satisfy and suffice – was coined by Economics Nobel Laureate Herbert Simon. In his Nobel acceptance speech, he said, "Decision makers can satisfice either by finding optimum solutions for a simplified world, or by finding satisfactory solutions for a more realistic world. Neither approach, in general, dominates the other, and both have continued to co-exist in the world of management science."[16]

This is why the SLASOG Framework includes *optimize*. Data-driven impact requires:

* Identifying high-leverage empirically valid mechanisms

* Aligning everything to these high-leverage opportunities

* Simplifying everything else by removing all irrelevant information

* Optimizing for the greatest returns

Turing Award-winning Dutch computer scientist Edsger W Dijkstra formulated this aptly: "The purpose of abstraction is not to be vague, but to create a new semantic level in which one can be absolutely precise."[17]

In an AI hype- and snake oil-filled world, it is not surprising that people are evolutionarily hardwired to pick the sevens due to satisficing. What satisficing does not take into account, though, is the power law in the underlying outcomes. A ten might have a slightly lower consensus probability of success than a seven, but if a ten has a 1,000× outcome in the case of success, its expected return is probably at least 100× the expected return of the consensus seven or the politically even safer five. This is why by repeatedly picking sevens, fives, or tens, the opportunity costs of 100× compound and lead to power law-style declines of the politically safe decisions.

Customer demand, unfair non-digital advantage, and counter-positioning

For most of human history, and until the end of World War II in several countries, the world was massively supply-constrained. The biggest challenge for businesses was establishing consistent, safe, and inexpensive supply. From Adam Smith to business thinkers in the early twentieth century, all the focus was on optimizing supply. The legendary Peter Drucker is the first business thinker to shift from supply and focus on the customer and on demand, when he famously wrote in *The Practice of Management* that the purpose of a business is to create and keep a customer.[18]

The evolution of value creation from leveraging supply to leveraging demand runs like this:

- Manufacture or supply the product
- Distribute the product
- Own the customer relationship and transaction
- Personalize the product or service
- Influence purchase intent and customer behavior

Does each of your customers buy the same products at the same time with the same frequency from you? If that is the case, then there is no hidden leverage in your customer demand. Fortunately, though, it is near impossible that this applies to you – a uniform distribution is extremely rare in business. When there are additive processes at play, like for example the distribution of T-shirt sizes in a population, the result is often a bell curve. This means that most sales will be around size medium, and as you go the extremes XXS and XXL, there will be comparatively fewer sales.

Power laws

There are multiplicative processes – like word-of-mouth recommendation and network effects – that result in power laws. For example, if people love a book or movie and recommend it to their friends, and in turn, some of those friends recommend it forward, the resulting distribution is a power law. The concentration of well-served customer demand also leads to power laws. This is where the value you are delivering and the goodwill and delight you bring to your customers are concentrated in their densest form. Your biggest leverage is your customer demand.

Another example of hidden power laws in your business is probably in your marketing and distribution channels. A few channels probably drive the majority of your inbound leads and customers. This could be because the density of your ideal customer profile is best reached through these channels, or because these channels allow for better propagation of word-of-mouth recommendation through network effects.

Leveraging power laws has an evolutionary basis too, since species that thrive over long periods have a high conversion rate for finding food. Your ability to find concentration in value delivery for your customers is critical not just for growth but also for survival over time.

Find the power laws that matter. Leverage the assets from your legacy business to build new digital data-driven assets.

Leveraging your customer demand

If you're in a legacy business that moves physical products, like Walmart in retail or Instacart in groceries, then the flow of customer demand data – in the reverse direction of the flow of physical products – is useful. You buy physical products from your suppliers and fulfill customer demand for those products. This in effect means that you have proprietary granular data on your customer demand, which is extremely useful to your suppliers. Your suppliers could benefit hugely from your actionable insights on customer behaviors, needs, wishes, and more. The customers of your legacy business are the new suppliers of your new data-driven business, and the suppliers of your legacy business are the new customers of your data-driven business. This new data-driven business model is what Walmart and Instacart have successfully built out over the past decade.

Some airlines have leveraged the loyalty programs of their legacy air travel business to use customer behavior data, effectively becoming banks.[19] By partnering with payment providers and credit card companies, airlines monetize the miles they can create at will in their proprietary loyalty programs into new direct revenue streams. These new data-driven, revenue-generating assets can then be used as collateral for securing loans or investments. By leveraging the proprietary assets of their loss-making or low-profitability legacy air travel businesses to create new, high-margin, data-driven assets, airlines have successfully built hybrid businesses that combine air travel with personalized financial services and other relevant product offerings.

Leveraging your unfair advantages

Leverage also comes from identifying and exploiting your digital disadvantages, or more importantly, your non-digital advantages. Walmart used its vast network of retail stores to build detailed, data-driven, granular user journeys of the hybrid experience and of the behavior of its customers, both online and in its physical stores. When Amazon and other pure-play e-commerce companies started gaining market share, the physical footprint of Walmart stores was labeled a liability and a huge disadvantage. However, by leveraging the unique proprietary data of their stores, Walmart was able to gain an even deeper understanding of its customers' behavior and experiences.[20] Similarly, Bajaj Finance grew its consumer lending business by stationing employees at physical stores where people would come to purchase durable goods like household appliances. Its physical presence in stores allowed the company to meet customers at the physical point of purchase to offer them financing options.[21]

Counter-positioning

Another source of leverage comes from asking yourself what your company can do, such that if others copied you, they would incur massive costs to their existing business. This is *counter-positioning*. Your competitors clearly know your approach is better, but they cannot compete with you because it would cannibalize their existing business.

Netflix, for example, introduced a subscription-based model without late fees, providing customers with unlimited DVD rentals by mail. In contrast, larger incumbent Blockbuster's business model was based on earning revenue from late fees and physical stores. Blockbuster's customers hated late fees and joyously moved to Netflix. Even though all this was happening in plain sight, Blockbuster struggled to counter because that would have resulted in it cannibalizing its existing revenue. A similar counter position scenario unfolded when Netflix started streaming services. Blockbuster would have been forced to write off and shut its revenue-generating physical stores to be able to effectively compete against Netflix in the streaming game.[22]

Similarly, traditional large insurance companies in Germany relied on networks of sales agents and brokers to sell their products. This was very expensive as the broker networks involved huge distribution costs. When HUK24 started as a direct insurer, it focused narrowly and exclusively on providing a streamlined, online-only experience to cost-conscious, internet-savvy insurance buyers.[23] This allowed them to pass on the savings from not having a broker network directly to customers, through cheaper policies. Narrowing focus on a small customer group in the short term allows for greater compounding via a flywheel, which allows for more widening of the customer group in the long term. Now with the best value for money policies in the entire market, HUK24 attracts more customers who want the best deal and are used to the convenience of buying most things online.

This further highlighted the huge difference in price and experience between an online-only direct insurer like HUK24 and other legacy insurers. It is a classic case of counter-positioning, where a digital, data-driven entity can win against larger incumbents. Traditional competitors struggled to compete with their online-only direct insurers because it would have involved alienating their existing distribution network of brokers and agents, and would have affected their revenue in the short term. By keeping the HUK24 brand independent from the HUK-Coburg legacy brand, both insurers were able to grow and dominate the automotive insurance sector in Germany.

To summarize, here is how leveraging customer demand with legacy assets and counter-positioning is a highly effective data-driven approach to winning:

- **Capture existing demand:** The power of capturing existing demand by counter-positioning works best when it effectively solves a clear existing customer pain point that incumbents are unwilling or unable to address.

- **Short-term narrow focus, long-term wider growth:** Netflix started with a narrow focus on DVD rentals as a subscription without late fees, and HUK24 started with a narrow focus on customers looking for the cheapest insurance online. Over time, however, with a market-leading offering, counter-positioned companies can expand into broader customer groups.

- **Legacy business cannibalization:** Larger, traditional competitors are aware that the counter-positioned strategy is better but are constrained by their existing business models and revenue streams. They are thus unable to respond decisively.

- **Long-term compounding:** Once established, a counter-positioned leveraged flywheel compounds value creation for customers at a phenomenal rate and is thus very hard to dislodge by competitors due to the self-reinforcing competitive advantage.

Productization for leveraged value delivery

Elizabeth Grace Saunders developed the INO framework for prioritization in general.[24] Product leader Shreyas Doshi then adapted it into a useful framework for identifying leverage and non-leverage opportunities, which he called the LNO Framework.[25] The idea is to identify which tasks should be allocated more time, craft, and effort, and which tasks should be actively starved of those factors to maximize impact. The LNO Framework categorizes tasks into the buckets:

- Leverage – approximately 10× your impact

- Neutral – approximately 1× your impact

- Overhead – less than 1× your impact

In this context, 10× or 1× is a multiple of the time, craft, and effort invested in the task.

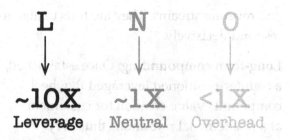

The LNO Framework[26]

After the LNO categorization, the goal is to minimize opportunity costs while allocating resources to the highest-impact tasks, by:

- Focusing most resources on the leverage tasks to do a great job

- Putting some resources into doing neutral tasks at an adequate level

- Actively starving overhead tasks of resources to get them done without any regard to improving quality

Value creation across paradigms

We started this chapter by discussing how sevens kill companies because of opportunity costs. During the course of my career, I have regularly seen expensive data experts being asked to do work with a one-time payoff. I have also seen decision-makers justify these investments by focusing on the size of the one-time payoff. However, as discussed in this chapter, the focus should be on building highly leveraged assets that can compound over long periods.

How can the LNO Framework be adapted to the data-driven value-creation paradigm?

- **Value creation in the industrial paradigm** – in producing physical industrial goods – is scarcity-based and input-constrained, with constant marginal costs for replication and constant marginal costs for personalization. Value creation can therefore be calculated in a static framework that is not time-indexed.

- **Value creation in the digital paradigm** – in producing software – has zero marginal costs for replication but constant marginal costs for personalization. Value creation in the digital paradigm should thus be evaluated in a time-index manner by looking at the shape of the value creation curve.

- **Value creation in the digital data-driven paradigm** – in data-driven software – has zero marginal costs for replication and zero marginal costs for personalization. Value creation in the digital data-driven paradigm should therefore be evaluated as the rate of change of the time-index value creation curve.

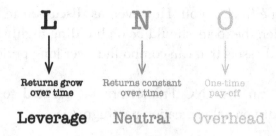

LNO Framework: Data Impact[27]

An example of leverage would be building a data-driven revenue-generating product. Such a product will have increasing returns over time, which leads to compounding of impact.

An example of neutral is optimizing a step in a work-flow. This usually leads to a change in the level of improvement, resulting in a constant return over time. This is valuable, but unlike with leverage, the return doesn't grow and compound.

An example of overhead is a one-time analysis of data in the format of a report that enables a deci-sion. Because this has a one-time return, irrespective of how large the return itself is, it is almost always smaller than something that is leveraged and that can compound over long periods.

Unfortunately, the easiest thing that most executives expect to create value is a detailed analysis of data pre-sented to a committee. In the data-driven paradigm, this kind of investment has the highest opportunity

costs. In very rare cases, where the analysis is necessary for existential reasons, it is satisfactory to do a
one-time analysis and report. In every other situation,
though, the opportunity costs are simply phenomenal.

Leveraged execution and the theory of special operations

As commander of Joint Special Operations Command
(JSOC), Admiral William McRaven organized and
led Operation Neptune Spear, which resulted in the
2011 killing of Osama bin Laden. Since McRaven
had worked for more than a decade solely on
counter-terrorism operations, he was given command
of all operational and execution decisions for the raid
by the then CIA director, Leon Panetta.

In 1993, at the Naval Postgraduate School, McRaven
wrote his master's thesis titled "The Theory of Special
Operations."[28] Special operations, by their very name,
are special or unique and have very diverse objectives,
environments, and contexts. McRaven's objective was
to study eight of the most seminal special operations
of the past century to determine the underlying principles that led to their successes. McRaven notes that
"Large forces are more susceptible to the frictions
of war. The principles of special operations work
because they seek to reduce warfare to its simplest
level and thereby limit the negative effects of chance,
uncertainty, and the enemy's will."

Relative superiority

Despite the underlying variations, a common theme across all special operations was that a smaller, specialized force gained a decisive advantage over a larger, more conventional opponent. McRaven explains that relative superiority relates to when an attacking force gains a decisive advantage over a larger enemy.

Achieving relative superiority does not guarantee the mission will succeed, but once relative superiority is achieved, the mission is essentially derisked. McRaven says that, while relative superiority doesn't guarantee success, it is necessary for success. To improve the chances of winning, it is therefore vital before any mission to determine the best way to achieve relative superiority.

In the case of an aircraft hijacking, for example, the point of relative superiority is achieved once the special forces team has entered the aircraft and neutralized the hijackers. The mission is not yet complete, and the hostages are not yet safely home, but the mission is derisked. The point of relative superiority is like an inflection point, after which things are more in control and less likely to go wrong.

When executing high-leverage initiatives, I always find it useful to identify the points of relative superiority and map them out as milestones on a roadmap. This helps in terms of resource allocation, as resources can be focused on achieving the next point of relative superiority. Once that is achieved, then all resources can be pivoted again to the next point of relative superiority. This allows fewer resources to be leveraged in a focused manner to repeatedly achieve greater results. Even if things go wrong, as they always will, the sheer leverage of this approach results in significantly better results than would be otherwise possible. Get your special forces ready to leverage data-driven impact for your customers!

DISCUSSION POINT: Leverage your assets and unfair advantage

Discuss these five questions with your team to identify your leverage:

1. What are the power laws in your customer demand and data?

2. How can you leverage the unique legacy assets of your business?

3. What is your unfair non-digital advantage, and how can you leverage it?

4. How can you use counter-positioning as leverage to grow your new data-driven business?

5. How can you productize the leveraged impact you deliver to your customers?

High leverage pioneers

The following two case studies illustrate how two legacy businesses, each more than half a century old, successfully leveraged their customer demand, unique non-digital advantage, and counter-positioning to build data-driven businesses around their legacy business brand.

CASE STUDY: High leverage pioneer – How HUK24 built a digital-first personalized insurance machine

In Germany most communication with insurance companies takes place by paper mail – completely crazy when compared with most other countries! It is antiquated and very annoying for anyone who is not used to constant, expensive paper mail. The reason for this, according to Dr Uwe Stuhldreier on the Digital Insurance Podcast, is that, in aggregate, the insurance sector in Germany has email addresses for only about 15% of its customers.[29] (Before investing in the latest AI trend, perhaps start by getting all the email addresses and mobile numbers of your customers.)

A rare exception is HUK24, which has email addresses for all its customers, and where the entire customer journey is a smooth, user-friendly online experience without the need for slow, irritating, wasteful paper mail.

Summary

HUK24 is the digital subsidiary of the German mutual insurer HUK-Coburg. HUK-Coburg was founded in 1933 and, as of 2024, has more than 13 million customers and in excess of 45 million contracts. It is the largest motor vehicle insurance company in Germany in terms of number of contracts. HUK24 has transformed the automotive insurance market by leveraging a fully digital, customer-obsessed, and cost-efficient business model. In a traditionally conservative industry, HUK24's highly leveraged approach – focus on digital simplicity, personalization, and the lowest policy premiums – has enabled it to outperform all other auto insurers in Germany. By 2024 HUK24 had captured a significant share of the direct insurance market, with well over 2 million customers and a cost ratio of just 5%, compared with the market average of 17%. This case study explores the leadership role of executives like Dr Uwe Stuhldreier and Detlef Frank, who drove HUK24's success over the past years of fast growth. It provides a highly leveraged actionable playbook for businesses aiming to innovate in legacy industries.

Context

HUK24 was founded in 2000 during the first dot-com bubble, as a subsidiary of HUK-Coburg. HUK24 was initially established to anticipate the growing demand for digital insurance solutions. By 2010 HUK-Coburg had a stronghold in the traditional insurance market, with more than 10 million policyholders. However, the rise of digital-first competitors and price-sensitive consumers began reshaping customer expectations. Traditional industry giants like Allianz Germany, burdened by higher cost structures and legacy systems, struggled to adapt.

HUK24 captured the market through its highly leveraged customer-obsessed execution based on its values "Digital. Einfach. Günstiger" ("Digital. Simple. Cheaper"). Unlike traditional insurance players, HUK24 operated without physical branches or intermediaries, and also without telephone support, instead offering customers a direct, online-only platform. The objective was clear: to capitalize on the growing shift toward digital shopping and lower operating costs while serving customer demands for simplicity, personalization, and transparency.

Challenges

Despite its early success, HUK-Coburg recognized emerging challenges in the automotive insurance sector. These included:

- **New competitors:** Price comparison portals like CHECK24 and upcoming InsurTechs were capturing market share by offering streamlined, user-friendly digital experiences.

- **Customer expectations:** Increasing demand for transparency, rapid service, and competitive pricing was reshaping consumer behavior because consumers were being shaped by their other online experiences like shopping for clothes, buying airline tickets, or streaming video.

- **Cost pressures:** Traditional insurers faced higher operating expenses due to agent commissions and brick-and-mortar operations, which limited their ability to offer competitive pricing on policies and premiums.

HUK24 was tasked with navigating these challenges to sustain growth and profitability, while maintaining its cooperative ethos of customer-centric service.

Methodology

HUK24's strategy centered on a highly leveraged digital-first, customer-focused approach:

1. **Leadership and vision**
   - Dr Uwe Stuhldreier, as a key architect of the strategy, championed the use of advanced analytics and real-time data management to streamline operations. His vision for a seamless customer experience drove innovations like automated contract renewals or one-click buy-purchase processes.
   - Detlef Frank ensured scalable, efficient back-end operations, actuarial pricing, and underwriting, enabling HUK24 to handle a growing customer base without compromising service quality.

2. **Customer-centric innovation**
   - Policy structures and transparent pricing were simplified, allowing customers to compare offerings easily without the need to speak with an insurance broker.
   - A pioneering AI Chatbot was deployed on the homepage to support customer queries and needs.
   - Reliance on third-party aggregators like CHECK24 was avoided, passing cost savings directly to consumers, thus compounding the flywheel of more customers leads to lower costs leads to lower premiums, which leads to more customers.

3. **Data-driven personalization**
   - This positioned HUK24 as a "customer-first" insurer, emphasizing trust, and leveraging the

respected HUK-Coburg brand along with the value and user experience of HUK24's brand.

- A personalized insurance engine to analyze customer behavior and tailor offerings was introduced, enabling one-click policy purchases similar to e-commerce platforms.

- Enhanced digital marketing strategies with intelligent programmatic advertising were implemented to effectively target price-sensitive consumers, who were the ideal customer profile for HUK24's market-leading policy premiums.

Outcomes

HUK24's strategy delivered impressive results.

- **Market share:** HUK24 dominated Germany's direct automotive insurance market, becoming the largest provider in this segment.

- **Cost leadership:** A cost ratio of 5% was achieved – far below the market average of 17% – enabling competitive pricing.

- **Customer base:** HUK24 gained well over 2 million policyholders, with sustained annual growth.

- **Profitability:** Strong margins were maintained despite competitive pricing, thanks to HUK24's low-cost model and high customer retention.

- **Customer satisfaction:** HUK24 matched or exceeded other insurers in satisfaction ratings, thanks to its user-friendly digital interface and responsive service.

In contrast, Allianz Germany faced challenges due to higher operational costs and slower adaptation to digital trends. While Allianz maintained a broad customer base, it struggled to compete effectively in the direct insurance space, where HUK24 excelled.

Key takeaways

1. **Customer-centricity is non-negotiable:** By prioritizing transparency, simplicity, and affordability, HUK24 built lasting trust with its customers. Businesses must adapt to evolving customer expectations to remain competitive.

2. **Leverage core strengths:** HUK24 benefited from HUK-Coburg's established brand and reputation while carving a distinct identity as a digital-first insurer. This balance of leveraging traditional strengths while innovating independently is critical for success.

3. **Embrace digital distribution:** HUK24's success underscores the importance of a digital-first approach in modernizing legacy industries. Automation and data-driven strategies are crucial for reducing costs and enhancing customer experiences.

4. **Leadership matters:** Visionary leaders like Stuhldreier and Frank demonstrated how executive commitment to a customer-obsessed, leveraged, aligned, and simplified strategy can drive optimized growth and organizational success.

Conclusion

HUK24's simplified, user-friendly, digital-first approach has revolutionized Germany's automotive insurance market over the past decade. By leveraging the assets of its legacy parent company, HUK-Coburg, and by adapting to new market needs through data-driven customer obsession, HUK24 showed that phenomenal value creation is possible, even in legacy industries. The clear vision and pragmatic rational leadership of Dr Uwe Stuhldreier and Detlef Frank were instrumental in navigating challenges and capitalizing on opportunities in the digital age.

As HUK24 continues to grow, its journey offers valuable insights for companies seeking to disrupt legacy industries. The lesson is clear: in an increasingly digital world, a relentless focus on customer needs, coupled with leveraging the unfair incumbent advantage of legacy assets and brands, is the key to sustained success.

CASE STUDY: Revolutionizing retail – How Walmart transformed data into dollars

A friend of the Instacart CRO and ex-Amazon VP Seth Dallaire reached out to him on behalf of Walmart, who were seeking alternative revenue streams.[30] Seth Dallaire said he would be happy to speak with Walmart US President and CEO John Furner or Walmart Inc. President and CEO Doug McMillon. In the call, Seth Dallaire asked John Furner if he was serious about building these alternative revenue streams. His reason for asking this was to ensure he would have full air cover to execute on building a layer of data-driven revenue-generating ventures on top of the core retail business. He had a lot of scar tissue from Amazon and knew such change was hard, and he was ready to fight the fight, but he knew it was impossible to pull through without complete and absolute air cover and alignment.

Summary

Walmart, the global retail giant, has successfully redefined its business model by leveraging its extensive data assets to build innovative digital data-driven ventures like Walmart+, Walmart Connect, and Walmart Data Ventures. This transformation, led by visionary executives like Dallaire, Furner, and McMillon, has positioned Walmart as a leader not just in retail but also in data-driven advertising and subscription services. By 2023 these digital ventures would contribute significantly to Walmart's diversified revenue streams and be growing at double-digit rates. This case study explores how Walmart's unique legacy market position, vast customer base, and new data capabilities enabled its remarkable success, providing valuable insights for businesses aiming to leverage their legacy assets for phenomenal data-driven value creation.

Context

Founded in 1962, Walmart is a dominant force in retail, by 2019 serving more than 230 million customers weekly across 10,500 stores across 24 countries. Known for its Everyday Low Prices strategy, Walmart's success was built on operational efficiency and an unparalleled supply chain. However, by the late 2010s, Walmart faced intensifying competition from Amazon in e-commerce and digital advertising. Amazon's ability to monetize its platform through advertising and subscription services highlighted opportunities Walmart had yet to fully capitalize on.

Recognizing these challenges, Walmart embarked on a journey to rethink and evolve its business by leveraging its extensive customer data and retail network. This shift was driven by a strategic emphasis on digital innovation and customer-centric solutions, under the leadership of Doug McMillon, Walmart's CEO since 2014. He was supported by key hires like Seth Dallaire, who brought extensive experience from VP at Amazon and CRO at Instacart.

Challenges

Despite its scale, customer reach and relationships, Walmart lagged behind Amazon and other tech giants in monetizing its digital and data-driven capabilities. Key challenges included:

- **Lack of diversified revenue streams:** Walmart's reliance on traditional retail left it vulnerable to margin pressures in an increasingly competitive traditional retail market.

- **Underutilized data assets:** Walmart's massive trove of customer data remained largely untapped as a source of value creation, revenue, and growth.

- **Subscription market pressure:** Amazon Prime's success underscored the need for Walmart to develop a compelling subscription service to drive loyalty, convenience, and engagement.

- **Advertising opportunities:** Competitors like Amazon and Google dominated the digital advertising market, leaving Walmart with minimal market share, despite its vast customer base.

Methodology

Walmart's transformation into a data-driven business was anchored in leveraged investments into its unfair non-digital physical in-store advantage, massive customer demand, and legacy assets, along with a clear and bold leadership and vision.

1. **Walmart+**
   - Launched in 2020, Walmart+ was designed as a subscription service offering free shipping, fuel discounts, and other benefits. It competed directly with Amazon Prime, aiming to enhance customer loyalty and frequency of shopping.
   - Walmart leveraged its vast store network to create a hybrid model blending online and offline experiences. For example, Walmart+ members could benefit from same-day delivery powered by local stores.

2. **Walmart Connect**
   - Walmart Connect, the company's advertising arm, enabled brands to reach millions of customers through targeted ads on Walmart's website, app, and in-store displays.
   - Under Dallaire's leadership, Walmart Connect focused on building advanced analytics and self-service advertising tools, enabling marketers to optimize campaigns using Walmart's first-party data.

3. **Walmart Data Ventures**
   - Walmart Data Ventures commercialized Walmart's proprietary data by providing insights to brands and suppliers.
   - Products like the Luminate platform offered detailed analytics on customer behavior, helping partners optimize inventory and marketing strategies.

4. **Leadership and vision**
   - McMillon emphasized innovation and collaboration, ensuring Walmart's digital

ventures aligned with its core mission of helping customers save money.

- Dallaire, as chief revenue officer, brought expertise from Amazon as well as Instacart and built Walmart's advertising and data monetization initiatives.

- Furner, CEO of Walmart US, focused on integrating physical and digital experiences, ensuring Walmart's stores played a central role in its omnichannel strategy.

Outcomes

Walmart's data-driven transformation yielded impressive results:

- **Revenue growth**
  - Walmart Connect has achieved a double-digit year-over-year increase in US advertising revenue in the past years, reaching billions in annual revenue.
  - Walmart+ subscriptions grew steadily, with millions of members reported over the past years, contributing to higher customer retention and lifetime value.

- **Profitability**
  - Digital ventures like Walmart+, Walmart Connect, and Walmart Data Ventures became high-margin businesses, diversifying Walmart's income streams beyond traditional retail, and increasingly driving half of its growth.

- **Customer engagement**
  - Walmart+ members shopped more frequently and spent more per visit compared with non-members, due to stronger brand loyalty.

- Personalized advertising campaigns through Walmart Connect drove higher conversion rates for brands, strengthening Walmart's advertising appeal.

• **Competitive positioning**
  - Walmart's hybrid model, combining digital innovation with its physical store network, created a unique advantage over Amazon.

Key takeaways

1. **Leverage core assets:** Walmart's extensive store network and vast customer base were critical enablers of its digital ventures. Businesses should identify and leverage their unique strengths to drive innovation.

2. **Invest in leadership:** Bringing in experts like Seth Dallaire accelerated Walmart's learning curve in data-driven businesses. Companies should prioritize hiring leaders with the right expertise for new initiatives.

3. **Focus on customer experience:** Walmart+ succeeded by addressing specific customer pain points such as delivery speed and fuel costs. Understanding and solving customer needs remains vital for loyalty.

Conclusion

Walmart's transformation from a retail powerhouse to a digital data-driven behemoth demonstrates the potential of leveraging data to diversify and enhance business models. The leadership of Doug McMillon, Seth Dallaire, and John Furner was instrumental in this journey, driving high-leverage initiatives that now serve as benchmarks for the industry.

As Walmart continues to innovate, its success underscores the importance of adaptability, customer focus, and leveraged use of data in building resilient and fast-growing businesses. For other legacy companies, Walmart's insane success story offers a compelling blueprint for thriving in a rapidly evolving digital data-driven paradigm.

THREE

Align

American author and motivational speaker Zig
Ziglar is reported to have said that it doesn't matter how much power, brilliance, or energy you have
unless you harness those factors and focus them on a
specific target to accomplish your full potential. This
chapter explores the benefits of aligning everyone and
everything to your leveraged goals, unifying organizational efforts around clear, impactful goals.

Your raison d'être

Your customers don't care about your revenue and
profitability. Most importantly, your customers are
the sole source of your revenue and profitability
of your business. With this in mind, does it even

remotely make any sense to decide which digital data-driven initiatives to invest in and scale, based on some vague notion of future cash flows, revenue, or profitability?

In this chapter, let's focus on combining your leverage into alignment. With leverage you have identified how to amplify your data-driven impact, and with alignment you can now focus that impact on the one thing that matters to your customers. Alignment is the tip of the spear. It takes the force of your leverage and concentrates it, resulting in the greatest impact possible.

The foundation of alignment has to be your raison d'être – the reason for the existence of your business. This ensures your business goal is aligned to your customers, and that every employee in your business is aligned to that goal. The objective is to understand the value delivered and impact achieved for your customers, to quantify that value, and to use that quantified value as a rallying point to align everyone to this one existential goal.

Your North Star metric

Sean Ellis, considered the inventor of *growth hacking*, says a North Star metric should capture the value delivered to customers as this is the only driver of long-term sustained growth.[31] Other easier-to-measure quantities like revenue, number of customers, profitability, etc, are vanity metrics that should be avoided. Sean Ellis makes a clear distinction between leading and lagging indicators. A North Star metric should be a leading indicator that directly reflects the value delivered to customers, as this is the right predictor for future growth. The reason for this is that leading indicators are actionable and serve as an alignment mechanism for people. Lagging indicators on the other hand measure the outcomes retrospectively and are thus not actionable. A North Star metric will have a direct relationship to lagging indicators like revenue and customer retention.

Matt Lerner, author of *Growth Levers and How to Find Them*, links the definition of a North Star metric with the jobs-to-be-done approach of Anthony Ulwick.[32] The key question Lerner recommends asking is *How do we measure the value delivered to our customers?*, then mapping the response to concrete quantifiable user behavior that reflects the value delivered.

Here is a high-level four-step process to define a North Star metric:

1. **Understand customer impact:** Identify what value delivered and success look like for your customers. To do this, analyze customer data, customer interviews, and surveys to determine the key "aha moments" when your customers experience the unique value you provide to them.

2. **Quantify impactful behaviors:** Pick a leading indicator that correlates with measurable changes to user behavior – changes that drive lagging indicators like user retention, revenue, or recommendation.

3. **Align with financial targets:** Ensure that your leading indicator capturing customer impact is aligned with your financial targets. For example, if growth is the goal, customer recommendation and referral should be in focus. If engagement is a goal, product usage should be in focus. Consistency between the North Star metric defined and the financial targets is critical to ensure alignment in incentives and execution for your teams.

4. **Clarity, simplicity, and consistency:** The North Star metric should be clearly defined, simple, and understood by every person in your organization. It should also be robust enough to remain relevant as the company scales for a while – changing a North Star metric frequently is counterproductive and dangerous.

Commander's intent and metrics that matter

Behaviors and evolutionary factors often cloud decision-making, judgment, and clear rational thinking at the individual level. As the size of a group grows, so does the lack of clear rational thinking, due to emergent behavior like herd mentality, groupthink, and fragmented interest groups and communities. Interestingly, large groups of people are typically capable of acting rationally only when they are either under grave threat of survival or after they have exhausted all other alternatives. A commander's intent, combined with metrics that matter, can make teams act intelligently, independently, and with adaptability, even without the threat of survival or exhaustion.

Commander's intent

Commander's intent is a military practice, where leaders communicate a clear and overarching goal for a mission. This allows all teams to act autonomously but with accountability, where the commander's intent serves as a litmus test to align all decisions to the same goal. Success is measured against achieving the mission's intent, not merely in following a roadmap or orders. This is extremely useful in uncertain, dynamically changing environments, where adaptability with clarity and decentralized decision-making are critical for success.

A typical commander's intent has the following elements:

- **Goal:** One sentence on the mission's purpose (who, what, when, where, and why)

- **End state:** Detailed description of the mission's goal and ideal outcome

- **Sequence:** High-level phases, along with required resources and team outcomes

- **Initial state:** The empirical basis and rationale on which the mission is conceived

- **Key decisions:** Critical decisions that might need to be made during the mission

- **Antigoals:** Undesired outcomes that include the opposite of the end state

- **Constraints:** Guidelines on the environment, or restrictions on the use of resources

In summary: commander's intent helps to ensure everyone involved knows their mission and the overall vision of how the mission is to be executed.[33] This allows people to assess the scope within which they can operate and the types and levels of risks that are acceptable. In turn, leaders can expect that members should know their work better, do their work better, and collaborate better.

According to the US Marine Corps University, Napoleon kept an old, illiterate soldier on his staff, who would be read all written plans and commander's communications before they were issued. Napoleon would task the soldier with explaining the plan or communication, and if the explanation wasn't satisfactory, Napoleon would make sure the missive was rewritten.[34] Impact gets diluted through poor communication and transmission. Napoleon understood the importance of effectively scaling commander's intent to his troops.

Your North Star metric is your strategic anchor and aligns everyone to your purpose. Commander's intent gives you a framework to align distributed, autonomous, and empowered teams to execute in the best possible way towards a goal. Let's look next at how you can bridge the overarching North Star metric strategic anchor with the execution-focused commander's intent, delivering measurable outcomes at the organizational level.

Metrics that matter

Metrics that matter are the underlying quantified and actionable elements of your North Star metric.[35] If your North Star metric is your overall health and fitness, the metrics that matter are your vitals, body composition, blood sugar, cholesterol, VO2 max, resting heart rate, etc. In business, metrics that matter are the quantitative operational drivers defined at the team level to allow teams to execute towards the North Star metric, by being team-specific, granular, and actionable, and focusing on short- to mid-term goals. Metrics that matter give teams a framework to define quantifiable and actionable metrics that allow them to contribute directly to the North Star metric.

Here are some important characteristics of metrics that matter:

- **Alignment with North Star metric:** They have a consistent and combined direction of force.

- **Actionability:** They enable decision-making and quantify progress.

- **Simplicity:** They are easy to define, understand, and communicate across teams.

- **Focus on outcomes, not outputs:** They measure impact instead of activity.

- **Continuous relevance:** They adapt and evolve to the changing environment and needs.

Combining commander's intent with metrics that matter allows you to keep your teams aligned to the highest leverage opportunities while scaling your organization. The format, frequency, and style of meetings and team rituals from your company culture is something you can then leverage and align using the North Star metric, commander's intent, and metrics that matter.

High-stakes historical example

Sometimes it feels difficult to commit to one clear goal, but zooming out of your day-to-day business and putting yourself in a high-stakes scenario helps do that.

It's May 1940, and the Nazis have just invaded France. Try putting yourself in the shoes of Vannevar Bush, dean of the MIT School of Engineering; president of Carnegie Institution for Science; and overall a financially secure scientist, thanks to the commercial success of the companies he helped start and the technologies he brought to market.

Bush had seen the inadequate capabilities of the US military during World War I and was concerned that the technological superiority of the Nazis would inevitably lead to a US defeat if nothing hugely impactful was done right away. Bush identified the problem as the lack of effective collaboration between the US military and the scientific, civilian, and academic establishments. He was also keenly aware of the inferior quality of US Air Force aircraft and their engines. He had been appointed vice chairman of the National Advisory Committee for Aeronautics (NACA), NASA's predecessor. The chairman was unwell, and Bush, as acting chairman, struggled to convince senators of the importance of investing in military R&D. He eventually succeeded and was instrumental in setting up multiple research centers.

Vannevar Bush and military modernization

Bush quickly realized that getting developments via committees through discussions and consensus building was too slow to succeed in military modernization, especially given the pace at which the Axis powers were gaining ground. The stakes were too high. Bush therefore decided to approach President Roosevelt directly. He got Roosevelt's uncle, Frederic Delano, to set up a meeting with the president. Bush decided to keep the meeting simple, focusing on a decisive ask. He took a single piece of paper to the meeting, and within fifteen minutes Roosevelt signed it with "OK – FDR." That's how the National Defense Research Committee was born, and it was soon merged into the Office of Scientific Research and Development (OSRD), of which Bush became the director. Vannevar Bush was now the most empowered and influential US scientist, with a direct reporting line to President Roosevelt.

If you run and operate your own business, then you are simultaneously Bush and Roosevelt, and you need less than fifteen minutes to decide to start on your journey of data-driven value creation. If, like Bush, you're an executive or operator, then go with a clear, simple, and high-leverage pitch to the business owner and get them to sign off in fifteen minutes like Roosevelt. When the stakes are high, it is better to be less deliberative and more decisive. Mistakes will be made, but when the opportunity cost of inaction is survival, then all mistakes will also be forgiven.

If you are the Vannevar Bush of your company, how about you take this book and this anecdote to the Roosevelt of your business?

If you are the Roosevelt of your company, can a Vannevar Bush from your organization come to you and get prompt approval to act?

Conflicting objectives between core business and new initiatives

The main problem Bush faced was the fundamentally different natures of the US military and the scientific community. The military was a hierarchical command-and-control organization that valued predictability over uncertainty and reliability over experimentation, and where risk-taking was discouraged. The scientific community, on the other hand, was a diverse, decentralized network of researchers that sought the unknown and enjoyed experimentation, and where risk-taking and failures were encouraged as steps on the path to discovery. It would have been meaningless, irresponsible, and futile to try to merge these two disparate groups.

Bush did not adopt a spray-and-pray approach. He did not ask military leaders to brainstorm for narrow technological use cases to help them win the war. He also didn't start an across-the-board, multiyear technology-transformation initiative to transform the army into a tech organization by trying to boil the ocean. These approaches would have most likely had failure rates of more than 90% and led to crushing defeat. The silver lining to high stakes and a war for survival is that it can lead to good decision-making and resource allocation. Let's look at Vannevar Bush's approach.

1. A clear North Star to innovate with purpose for measurable results

Bush made sure that everyone – from military cadets and junior scientists all the way up to President Roosevelt – was aligned to one clear North Star: to win the war. Every decision that was made was prioritized by asking the question, *Will doing this help us win this war?* This led to innovation with purpose and to achievement of measurable results.

Some prioritization and resource allocation decisions made by Bush were very controversial. When mathematician Norbert Wiener asked Bush for funds to build an electronic computer in September 1940, Bush declined, arguing that the invention would not be ready fast enough to be used to win the war. A few years later, in 1943, Norbert Wiener did get funding and built the first general-purpose electronic computer by the end of 1945, shortly after the war ended. Due to the delayed funding, Bush's prediction turned out to be right, but it was probably a mistake not to have approved Wiener's request in 1940.

2. Centralized, autonomous leadership structure

You can afford to make a couple of mistakes if you get the most fundamental high-leverage decisions right. Essentially, they are all that matters. Centralizing critical decision-making, prioritization, resource allocation, and coordination, while giving scientists the autonomy to innovate within well-defined scopes in close collaboration with the military, was the structure that allowed rapid impact on the battlefield. This highlights the importance of centralized coordination with decentralized execution.

3. Organizational silos, with a focus on mission-driven, project-oriented goals

By breaking down barriers between the military, academic scientists, and private sector entities, Bush created an environment that encouraged information flow and collaboration. This approach highlights the importance of overcoming institutional silos to foster innovation. Bush also aligned scientific research with practical, mission-oriented goals, ensuring that projects were aligned with the military's needs. This emphasizes the importance of setting clear, achievable objectives with measurable outcomes.

Bush created cross-functional teams of scientists and soldiers, which focused on solving some of the mission-critical problems faced on the battlefield. In the early years of the war, Nazi U-boats would form wolf packs of submarines to attack Allied shipping lanes in the Atlantic, with devastating consequences.

OSRD got teams of scientists and navy aviators working closely together and even made scientists fly out on sorties with navy pilots. Not only was the radar and sonar technology required to detect submarines invented within thirty months, it was even developed into usable products for navy pilots. Early instances of sonar and radar equipment on aircraft were technically sound but practically impossible for pilots to use, as they involved intricate calculations and fine-tuning of equipment while flying the aircraft of that period. User-friendly dashboards of easy-to-calibrate knobs and measurements were therefore developed to make the use of sonar and radar technology feasible in warfare. The results are dramatically clear when tracking the ratio of Allied ships sunk to Nazi U-boats lost from 1939 to 1945:

- 1939: 9 U-boats lost, 222 Allied ships sunk, ratio ~ 25:1

- 1940: 22 U-boats lost, 471 Allied ships sunk, ratio ~ 21:1

- 1941: 35 U-boats lost, 432 Allied ships sunk, ratio ~ 12:1

- 1942: 87 U-boats lost, 1,155 Allied ships sunk, ratio ~ 13:1

- 1943: 237 U-boats lost, 588 Allied ships sunk, ratio ~ 2.5:1

- 1944: 249 U-boats lost, 132 Allied ships sunk, ratio ~ 0.5:1

- 1945: 153 U-boats lost, 56 Allied ships sunk, ratio ~ 0.3:1[36]

4. Lessons from high-stakes execution for your business

Boiling the ocean does not work. Technology for technology's sake is a meaningless goal. Taking your existing business that is focused on operational excellence, and turning it into a creative, risk-seeking, experimentation-oriented organization is incoherent and will have disastrous consequences. Within the same organization, you can't have goals that are in conflict. At any given point in time, and for a given set of people, you can either optimize for reliability, lack of errors, and operational excellence; or focus on creativity, experimentation, and developing new solutions.

Let's summarize the broad principles that work for winning in high-stakes settings:

1. Align everyone to a clear North Star.

2. Innovate with purpose for measurable results.

3. Establish a centralized fast-approval leadership structure, with decentralized execution and accountability.

4. Prioritize impact over activity, do a few high-leverage things right, and the rest will not matter.

5. Bridge organizational silos and align teams to common mission-driven goals.

For a deeper look at this period and Vannevar Bush's contributions, in the context of how organizations can succeed at radical breakthrough innovations, explained through the lens of phase transitions, read the excellent book *Loonshots* by Safi Bahcall.[37]

DISCUSSION POINT: Align on value creation and impact

Discuss these five questions with your team to align your company right away:

1. What is your North Star metric, and is your entire organization aligned to it?

2. Have you established a centralized, fast-approval leadership structure, with decentralized execution and accountability?

3. Do you use commander's intent to empower your teams to execute autonomously with complete alignment?

4. Do you use metrics that matter to align all your teams to your North Star metric?

5. Are your teams incentivized and evaluated on high-leverage impact and outcomes instead of easier-to-measure activity?

Aligned par excellence

The first of the two case studies below illustrates how a new company, by ensuring complete alignment to customers, built a successful data-driven, diversified powerhouse across multiple legacy industries.

The second shows how a legacy manufacturing business that is almost 150 years old successfully pivoted to become a B2B vertical software conglomerate by aligning to one key metric.

CASE STUDY: Revolutionizing energy – How Greg Jackson aligned Octopus Energy Group to build a diversified growth powerhouse

After having completed some good work, Octopus Energy's newly appointed director of marketing asked who should sign it off. The reply from founder and CEO Greg Jackson was probably unexpected but certainly the best that any ambitious and entrepreneurial operator could wish for. Jackson told the director that they needed to take responsibility for the work. Jackson added that if the director was worried about something being wrong or getting the company into trouble, they should seek advice or a legal opinion, but that solely they could take responsibility and sign it off.[38]

Jackson characterizes his responsibility as making sure no one can do anything that would be an existential threat to the company. Short of that, he wants people to get used to the idea that things will go wrong from time to time. Most often, annoying processes in businesses are created by someone trying to do the right thing and covering for it if something goes wrong. That creates unnecessary clutter and complexity and reduces the adaptability of the organization.

The culture Jackson has built at Octopus Energy is one that combines freedom with responsibility. The objective is decentralized execution with few process overheads, while ensuring high levels of rigor and discipline in decision-making. This is not easy and requires relentless effort.

Summary

Octopus Energy Group, founded in 2015 by Greg Jackson, grew rapidly in several different legacy industries like energy, infrastructure, and mobility by aligning the organization to one clear vision, as well as creating a customer-first, technology-driven business model. With a vision of making energy fair, clean, and simple for all using technology, Jackson unified all subsidiaries under a singular mission.

As of 2024, under its retail brand, Octopus has more than 7.7 million households as customers across multiple markets; a valuation of USD 9 billion; and leading positions in renewable energy, electric vehicle (EV) infrastructure, and global energy retail. This case study examines how Jackson's leadership aligned diverse businesses across different sectors to drive unparalleled growth and impact in traditionally legacy asset-heavy, slow-growth industries.

Context

Before Octopus Energy, the energy sector was characterized by high barriers to entry, opaque pricing, and a lack of customer-centricity. Dominated by incumbent large utilities with aging infrastructure, customers faced limited choices and inconsistent service. Meanwhile, the urgency of the climate crisis demanded a shift toward renewable energy and electrified mobility at a viable and affordable price point to drive adoption.

Jackson, with a background in marketing, technology, and entrepreneurship, decided to take this challenge head-on. Combining renewable energy generation, data-driven software, and exceptional customer service, Octopus Energy Group was born. The company expanded rapidly, launching subsidiaries in areas like solar, wind, electric vehicles, and energy as a service, while maintaining a cohesive, aligned strategy and the purpose of making energy fair, clean, and simple.

Challenges

Octopus Energy faced several challenges common to startups in legacy industries:

- **Fragmented business units:** Diversified ventures risked dilution of focus and inefficiency without a unifying aligned vision and strategy.
- **Slow industry dynamics:** Traditional energy markets were resistant to change due to regulatory complexity and entrenched large incumbents.
- **Customer expectations:** Consumers increasingly demanded sustainability and transparency but lacked trust in traditional energy providers.
- **Global scaling:** Entering diverse markets with varying regulatory requirements and consumer behaviors posed huge challenges in scaling.

Methodology

Jackson addressed these challenges through a leveraged and aligned approach:

1. **Visionary leadership and aligned purpose**
   - Greg Jackson's leadership helped redefine what a leveraged, aligned, and integrated sustainable energy and mobility company could be.

- The leadership and purpose articulated a clear mission: making energy fair, clean, and simple for all using technology.
- Freedom was combined with responsibility to align and decentralize decision-making and execution, but with a very rigorous and disciplined rationality.
- Building great teams is like building dry-stone walls: "Rather than forcing people into 'cuboids' and sticking them together in neat little rows, we take authentic humans, and find ways for them to fit together naturally to form a truly solid team."[39]

2. **Investment in leveraged tech assets**

   - Kraken, Octopus's proprietary technology platform, was built to optimize energy management and customer service. Krakenpowered energy retail, EV integration, and grid balancing across subsidiaries.
   - Kraken was licensed to other global utilities, generating revenue and fostering partnerships.

3. **Customer-centric innovations**

   - Pioneering flexible tariffs were introduced, including time-of-use pricing to incentivize energy usage during off-peak times.
   - EV-focused services were launched, including home charging solutions and renewable energy packages tailored to EV drivers.

4. **Partnerships and acquisitions**

   - Renewable energy assets were acquired, for example a 42MW solar farm near Dublin, to secure a sustainable energy supply.

- Octopus partnered with automakers to integrate energy solutions into EV ecosystems, like for example the partnership with Renault UK and Mobilize or with Stellantis to offer customers charging that is 100% renewable and hundreds of pounds cheaper per year.

Outcomes

Octopus Energy's approach resulted in phenomenal success:

- **Customer growth:** Expansion to more than 7.7 million households in the UK and beyond was achieved, with more than 100,000 net new customers monthly.[40]

- **Revenue and valuation:** A USD 9 billion valuation was attained, driven by strong revenue growth across subsidiaries and licensing deals for Kraken.

- **Operational efficiency:** Friction, waste, customer acquisition, and service costs were reduced through the Kraken platform, outperforming traditional utilities.

- **Sustainability leadership:** 100% renewable energy was supplied to all customers by managing more than 230 large-scale green energy projects with a combined capacity of 3.25GW of renewable generation capacity.

- **Global impact:** Nineteen countries were entered, which licensed Kraken to dozens of utilities, managing more than 50 million energy accounts worldwide.

Key takeaways

1. **Unified aligned mission drives synergy:** Octopus Energy's success highlights the importance of a

compelling mission to align diverse subsidiaries across multiple legacy industries to foster cohesion and synergies.

2. **Productized technology as a leveraged asset:** Proprietary data-driven software like Kraken can create competitive advantages, reducing costs and enabling scalability.

3. **Customer-centricity enhances trust:** By focusing on transparency, sustainability, and convenience, Octopus built lasting relationships in a historically low-trust, transactional utility sector.

4. **Adaptability and ownership leadership:** Centralized coordination and alignment, with decentralized execution, allowed Octopus Energy to adapt to changing market dynamics and grow rapidly.

Conclusion

Octopus Energy Group, under Greg Jackson's leadership, redefined what a digital data-driven energy and mobility company can be. By aligning subsidiaries under a shared vision and building leveraged customer-centric technology assets, the company revolutionized legacy industries like energy, infrastructure, and mobility by capturing demand, and aligning, simplifying, and optimizing supply.

As Octopus continues to expand and innovate, its story offers a roadmap for businesses seeking to disrupt entrenched sectors. With a steadfast focus on sustainability, efficiency, and customer empowerment, Octopus Energy is poised to continue to be a unique trailblazer in the global energy transition.

CASE STUDY: Transforming Roper Technologies – Brian Jellison's obsession with cash return on investment

In 2001 Brian Jellison became CEO of Roper Industries (later Roper Technologies), a manufacturer of industrial equipment.[41] Roper was originally founded in 1883 as the Florence-Wehrle Company, producing stoves and later lawnmowers. Over seventeen years, Jellison turned Roper into a high-growth, high-margin, vertical B2B software giant. His unrelenting focus on the KPI cash return on investment (CRI) aligned and simplified how the company operated, grew, and created value. CRI, expressed as a percentage, measures the cash flow generated by an investment, relative to the initial cash invested.

Summary

Roper Technologies' transformation under Jellison was remarkable because few companies had done this before. By aligning every decision – acquisitions, operations, and strategy – with CRI, Jellison steered Roper away from its traditional manufacturing roots into B2B vertical software and technology. This shift resulted in phenomenal growth in revenue, margins, and shareholder value. Roper's story offers a clear and successful blueprint for legacy businesses to adapt, evolve, and thrive in changing environments.

Context

In 1981 Roper Industries was founded, primarily as a manufacturer of fluid handling and industrial equipment. By the early 2000s Roper had stable but modest growth. However, Jellison saw the untapped potential for the company to pivot towards a capital-light, recurring-revenue model. His strategy was grounded in CRI – a metric that ensured investments maximized shareholder value by generating cash above the cost of capital.

Jellison's insight was that industrial equipment companies were capital-intensive and prone to cyclicality. By focusing on high-margin businesses like vertical software, Roper could reduce physical asset risk, grow faster, and deliver consistent returns.

Challenges

- **Capital intensity and no recurring revenue:** Roper's legacy manufacturing business had little to no recurring revenue, relying purely on project-based sales. Industrial equipment and machinery required huge investments in physical assets and working capital, reducing free cash flow.

- **Cultural resistance:** Turning a manufacturing company into a software-focused business required significant cultural and organizational change, pivoting the mindset from physical resource constraints and scarcity to abundance and growth.

- **Acquisition risks:** Jellison's strategy depended on acquiring high-quality businesses at reasonable valuations without overpaying by aligning everything to CRI.

Methodology

Jellison aligned Roper to CRI with absolute rigor and discipline:

1. **Relentless focus on CRI**
   - Jellison made CRI the guiding KPI for every decision, ensuring that acquisitions and

investments created substantial cash flow relative to their costs, thereby aligning the entire company to one clear goal.

- Operational decisions, such as resource allocation and efficiency improvements, were also measured against CRI.

2. **Pivoting to software**

- Roper began progressively acquiring vertical software companies in legacy industries like healthcare, transportation, and education. These companies had capital-light models with strong recurring revenues.

- The software businesses complemented Roper's legacy operations, leveraging existing customer relationships to grow further.

3. **Disciplined M&A strategy**

- Jellison prioritized buying companies with strong cash flow, market leadership, and predictable revenues. He avoided "transformational" vanity deals, focusing on smaller, accretive acquisitions.

- The company paid careful attention to integration, allowing acquired businesses to retain autonomy while adopting Roper's financial discipline and rigor concerning CRI alignment.

Outcomes

Roper's evolution from the industrial paradigm to the digital one yielded impressive results:

- **Growth and value creation**

  - By 2025 Roper's revenue had grown to over USD 6 billion, with more than half of its earnings coming from recurring revenues.[42]

- The company's market capitalization increased from USD 1.5 billion in 2001 to more than USD 58 billion by 2025.

- Operating margins improved from 20% to more than 30% during Jellison's tenure.

- Roper became a consistent performer in the S&P 500, delivering compounded annual returns of about 20% during Jellison's leadership.[43]

- **Resilience and recognition**

  - The shift to software and recurring revenue insulated Roper from economic cycles, creating a more stable earnings profile.

  - Roper's transformation inspired other industrial companies to explore software acquisitions, making it a benchmark for strategic reinvention.

Key takeaways

1. **Alignment for success**

   - Jellison's pivot to software demonstrated the power of aligning a legacy business with future growth trends.[44]

   - CRI provided a clear, actionable framework for decision-making, ensuring Roper prioritized high-value investments.[45]

2. **Disciplined acquisitions and leadership**

   - Roper's success highlights the importance of buying quality assets at the right price and enabling them to operate and grow effectively.

   - By giving acquired companies operational autonomy, Roper preserved entrepreneurial cultures while imposing financial discipline and CRI alignment to optimize and drive growth.

Conclusion

Brian Jellison's leadership at Roper Technologies exemplifies how a legacy company can reinvent itself by aligning to a clear strategic metric and focusing on value creation for customers. His rigorous approach to acquisitions, cultural alignment, and financial discipline turned Roper into a model of adaptability and growth, in a competitive, ever-evolving market undergoing massive paradigm shifts.

FOUR
Simplify

I love the quote from French writer Antoine de Saint-Exupéry, "Perfection is achieved, not when there is nothing more to add, but when there is nothing left to take away."[46] This chapter looks at the need to simplify in business, to reduce the cost of complexity, prevent collapse, and maximize leveraged returns.

Nuisance threshold and habit formation

From a supply perspective, books are physical products that have existed in various forms for hundreds of years. From a user experience perspective, books are an immersive, focused, linear experience – not unlike the digital products of today. Readers are now used to hyper-personalized experiences when streaming music or videos, or shopping online, and thus the expectations for personalized communication are rising further, even from physical products like books. Unlike with software, though, a book can't be changed or updated once it is shipped. In a strange way, therefore, while writing this book, I'm struggling in making a physical product that can't be modified after it is shipped. In some ways this aptly captures the challenge of data-driven value creation for legacy industries and products.

When buying a car – an expensive physical product with high switching costs – the purchase decision is based on evaluating the desirability of individual features and selecting the car with the best average features set. A physical product is usually purchased and experienced as an average of all its features.

A digital, data-driven product is a linear user journey, with low switching costs – people stop using the product and switch the moment the user experience drops below a certain threshold. Let's call that the *nuisance threshold*. Because switching costs for digital products are low, the average experience of the product features is irrelevant – the user has a nuisance threshold, after which they simply stop using your product. They therefore never experience the average value of your product.

Staying above the user's nuisance threshold is critical to getting the user to experience the average value of your product. However, it is not possible to know the nuisance threshold in advance for all users, and the threshold is usually not a static level either. One way to solve this is to try to build a *habit-forming product.*

The Hook Model

Behavioral engineer Nir Eyal, in his book *Hooked: How to build habit-forming products,* presents a coherent framework for digital habit formation.[47] The framework is based on four steps, which lead to iterative habit formation. This allows digital products to become stickier for users, thereby diluting the effect of the nuisance threshold. Habit formation is a useful binding and recovery mechanism that prevents users from leaving or switching digital products after hitting the nuisance threshold.

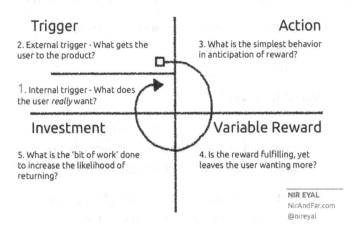

The Hook Model[48]

Language learning app Duolingo leveraged this approach by developing its Friends Streak feature, where users invite their friends and commit to doing at least one lesson every day.[49] Here's how the Friends Streak maps to the Hook Model:

1. **Trigger**

   – External trigger: Duolingo sends notifications like, *Your friend Emily just extended their streak! Keep your 74-day streak going with a lesson!*

   – Internal trigger: Users feel a sense of pride or competition, spurred by their streak progress or desire to outperform friends.

2. **Action**

   – The action is to complete a lesson to maintain your streak and stay in the game with friends.

   – *Duolingo* ensures the lessons are short and bite-sized, minimizing effort and maximizing motivation.

3. **Variable reward**

   – Tribe: Social validation comes from the user seeing their name climb the leaderboard or maintaining a streak alongside friends.

   – Hunt: Users "hunt" for rewards like gems, badges, and leaderboard recognition.

- Self: The streak itself provides a sense of satisfaction and reinforces the user's identity as a dedicated learner.

4. **Investment**

   - By maintaining streaks, users invest time and emotions, increasing their commitment to the app's learning goals.

   - Social features like inviting friends and competing on leaderboards further deepen this investment, making users less likely to abandon the app entirely.

The Hook Model can easily be applied when designing any digital or hybrid user experience. Combining your legacy products with digital products in a habit-forming loop along your user journey is an effective way to protect against the nuisance threshold.

Here are some principles to apply to every step of your user journey, to improve it iteratively:

- One clear goal to minimize cognitive load

- Actionable feedback with error correction

- Gamification and rewards

Digital and data-driven products have to be structurally simplified to be successful. Along with leverage and alignment, understanding simplification is critical to success.

Simplification to boost returns

In the last two chapters, you have learned how to:

- Identify high-leverage opportunities and align your team to them to maximize returns
- Find power laws in data from customer demand, using your unfair non-digital advantage and assets, to identify those high-leverage opportunities
- Look for opportunities for counter-positioning
- Further leverage these high-leverage opportunities through productization

Let us now look at the neutral and overhead categories in the Data Impact version of the LNO Framework and see how simplification can boost returns by keeping the costs of complexity under control.

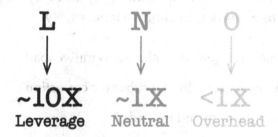

LNO Framework: Data Impact[50]

If an important decision is made regularly, and data is available for it, it makes sense to approach the decision as a neutral investment and focus on intelligent automation, to get a constant improvement in returns over time. The crucial point here is not just to automate the analysis or generate a forecast, but also to optimize the end-to-end outcomes of the decision. This will ensure that, after a one-time fixed investment in effort, a constant return is generated over time.

In terms of focus, effort, and investment, this means that leverage is an opportunity for sustained long-term value creation, and it therefore cannot be initially standardized or automated. Neutral tasks should be simplified, standardized, and reengineered. Overhead tasks should ideally be completely avoided and – only if unavoidable – be completed in a time-boxed manner or with a clear stopping criterion. Overhead tasks tend to quickly morph into wicked problems that lead to crippling opportunity costs.

We already spoke about leverage, and as discussed above, overhead should be ruthlessly shunned. Let's now look into neutral as people often try to automate an existing process without rethinking it from first principles. This is where simplification is critical to success.

Complexity and clutter

The right way to standardize and automate is to reengineer a process. Unfortunately, people often try to apply digital band-aids or algorithmic tapes to hold together or improve legacy processes. This results in lower efficiency and wasted optimization potential. Above all, it leads to ever-growing complexity. Complexity has an inherent cost that is not always explicit until it is too late.

No one willingly adds complexity, but complexity grows through narrow problem-solving over time. This is especially true for legacy businesses. Complexity grows, one problem-solving band-aid and patch at a time, until things are so brittle that they have to be demolished and rebuilt entirely. Growing in complexity is very seductive in the short term, but in the long term it leads to crippling costs, fragility, and decline. Complexity is easily spotted through clutter, and clutter always has high running costs. Clutter also leads to a lack of focus and clarity for teams, which leads to lower productivity and capped potential. This is why leverage and alignment need to be closely followed by simplification.

We dive deeper into the growing cost of complexity and risks of collapse towards the end of this chapter. Let's look first, though, into the role of process reengineering, such as in simplifying and standardizing processes in neutral investments. Reengineering through simplification and standardization of processes drives value creation in ways that people often can't foresee.

Reengineering processes

The age of software brought with it a paradigm shift to end-to-end process reengineering as well as the development of customer-centric user flows. In their seminal book *Reengineering the Corporation*, James Champy and Michael Hammer argued that incremental improvements were no longer sufficient in the fast-changing technology and globalizing landscape of the late twentieth century.[51] They recommended a fundamental rethink and radical transformation to achieve dramatic improvements.

Champy and Hammer embrace the ideas of process efficiency from their predecessors but reject the hierarchical and bureaucratic structures of the past. Their predecessors tried to innovate and optimize existing structures, and this is where Champy and Hammer emphasize the need for innovation and optimization while advocating a more radical rethink. Their work builds on the ideas of scientific management, human relations, and strategic planning, but Champy and Hammer also go well beyond these to create a new thesis. They argue that technological innovation and process efficiency can be achieved only by rethinking the corporate structure from first principles, because successfully leveraging new technology requires fundamental changes like breaking down silos, bureaucracies, and greater agility to achieve customer-centricity.

The underlying shift in worldview is discernible. Scientific management and related theories were based on a predictable, mechanistic, and compartmental view of the world, inspired by the corresponding paradigm in physics, chemistry, and the natural sciences. This worldview had been shattered by the second half of the twentieth century by the ideas of relativity and quantum mechanics. Most importantly, most of the advanced technology built in the second half of the twentieth century could not have been built without quantum mechanics or relativity.

Quantum mechanics and relativity rejected a worldview that was completely mechanistic, compartmentalized, entirely predictable, and independently measurable. Similarly, business process reengineering (BPR) by Champy and Hammer rejects a compartmentalized, specialized, and rigid corporate structure. They recommend integrated and cross-functional teams that are flexible, focused on customer needs, and able to adapt to market trends.

The transition from Newtonian physics to quantum mechanics and relativity is not incremental – rather it's a new paradigm and worldview. Similarly, Champy and Hammer reject incrementalism, instead embracing radical transformation and new technological realities. It is logically impossible to leverage the benefits of a new paradigm and worldview through small steps and incrementalism. To use an analogy from the history of astronomy: you can operate in a system centered around either the Earth or the sun; and most significantly, there is no step-by-step incremental path to go from a geocentric universe to a heliocentric one. Along with clarity of thought, courage is also needed to go from one paradigm to another.

Many of our pain points and problems in life and business arise from our primal urge to avoid unpredictability. In a world that is inherently unpredictable, we are constantly grasping for simplistic, predictable models and explanations. The quantum revolution forced physicists to embrace and theorize the irreducible uncertainty in nature. Champy and Hammer argue that businesses should embrace uncertainty and make sure it is reflected in their organizational structure by designing team structures that are customer-centric, flexible, and responsive. This brings us to why legacy industries that rely on extensive planning, based on a blueprint strategy and a deliberative consensus, are structurally set up to lose in a fast-moving disruptive macro environment where true uncertainty reigns.

Why adaptability beats planning

How can legacy businesses win in the digital data-driven paradigm within a fast-moving disruptive macro environment where true uncertainty reigns?

Most legacy businesses were founded and continue to operate in the industrial paradigm of predictable uncertainty. In this postwar industrial framework there is uncertainty, but that uncertainty is considered to be overall quantifiable. The future is therefore relatively well known and understood, and the job of strategic planning is to lay out a blueprint vision of the future that is precise enough to be used for discounted cash flow analysis.

A danger of this approach is that it makes executives think in binaries – the world is either certain, so things can be precisely predicted; or the world is uncertain, meaning things are completely unpredictable. This results in planning and capital budgeting processes based on point forecasts, where decision-makers are incentivized to ignore, gloss over, or bury the irreducible uncertainty of the world so that they can get their strategy, projects, and budget approved.

Misrepresenting uncertainty leads to strategies that don't protect from threats or leverage opportunities available from the irreducible uncertainty of the world. A great example of this is how boiling the ocean fits in with the notion, on one extreme, that everything is known and plannable over multiyear time horizons. On the other extreme, the world is considered so uncertain and entirely unpredictable that all analytical rigor is discarded, and a gut-feeling-based, random spray-and-pray approach is presented as the only solution. The most risk-averse decision-makers then choose to do nothing leveraged to delight the customer. Instead, at best they tend to focus on small, neutral process automation or cost-cutting. At worst they spend months on overhead one-time data analysis, modeling, or reports.

Surviving in true uncertainty

Under the assumptions of predictable uncertainty, strategic planning is based on a blueprint strategy. This blueprint is based on a vision of the future that can be reached by planning and forecasting through deliberative consensus, where input is provided by all the relevant functions such as sales, finance, and product. This involves some discussions about alternative scenarios to test how sensitive the forecast is to changes in certain pre-defined variables. In practice, though, the goal is to get committees of people converging, through extensive deliberation and compromise, on a commonly agreed future scenario.

Organizations that thrive in predictable uncertainty are by design bureaucratic, with slow, deliberative, politically viable, and consensus-based decision-making processes. This traditional strategic-planning process is designed to repeatedly pick the sevens that kill companies. Sevens usually kill companies slowly, but blueprint strategy is patently more dangerous and can kill companies much faster. The traditional strategic-planning process makes companies sluggish in adapting to the unknown and fast-changing environments that characterize true uncertainty.

Complexity and collapse

Anthropologist Joseph Tainter studied the decline of civilizations using concepts from network theory, complexity theory, and energy economics. In his 1988 book *The Collapse of Complex Societies*, he argues that as they iteratively solve problems, societies become ever more complex and that they subsidize this complexity with higher energy use.[52]

The military-industrial complex that was spawned in the era of Vannevar Bush grew and developed along Massachusetts Route 128. This came to be known in the early postwar years as the "Technology Highway," the "Magic Semicircle," and "Route 128." Proximity and collaboration with MIT, Harvard, and other leading Boston universities provided active exchanges of research and talent. Born out of the success and legacy of investments made during the peak of World War II, Route 128 thrived for several decades by inventing and developing cutting-edge industrial products. Over time, and with successive layers of problem-solving and optimization, this led to rigid hierarchical bureaucratic structures that operated independently through vertical integration. Route 128 excelled at making heavy industrial equipment and large computers.[53]

Silicon Valley, on the other hand, while also born close to the university ecosystem in California, was developed with less industrial legacy into smaller, less bureaucratic adaptable networks of companies. These collaborated extensively and regularly poached talent from one another, leading to a faster flow of ideas and more rapid cycles of experimentation and innovation. Silicon Valley's adaptable networked and flat organizational structures were ideal for capitalizing on the technological paradigm shift from large industrial machines and computing to modular scalable technologies like microprocessors, personal computers, and the internet.

Route 128 and Silicon Valley had similar roots, with proximity to excellent universities and large talent hubs, and Route 128 even had an incumbent advantage. However, with a change of technological paradigm, blueprint-based strategies with bureaucratic planning and consensus-based centralized decision-making became a massive liability for Route 128.[54] The cost of complexity of bureaucratic decision-making became too high to sustain, and since Route 128 could not adapt to the new paradigm, it went into rapid decline. Silicon Valley, meanwhile, with its adaptable, networked organizational structures, grew fast and became the ultimate home of innovation. Fast talent turnover, with employees moving quickly from one company to another, led to the faster spread of ideas and know-how and led to ever faster cycles of development and innovation.[55] Route 128 declined due to its bureaucratic blueprint consensus-based strategy suited for predictable uncertainty, while Silicon Valley won in a paradigm shift to true uncertainty thanks to its strategy of organizational adaptability.[56]

Is your business operating in predictable uncertainty or true uncertainty?

Do you need to get rid of your bureaucratic blueprint consensus-based strategy and pivot instead towards a strategy designed for true uncertainty by building a more adaptable organizational structure?

Tainter's theory characterizes strategic failures not just as poor management or bad decisions but also as a systemic problem, where the cost of maintaining complexity outpaces the resources or benefits derived from it. His perspective emphasizes simplifying, streamlining, and reducing unnecessary complexity as a way to help organizations survive over time.

To apply Tainter's ideas to your business:

- Prioritize adaptability by simplifying processes and flattening organizational structures to ensure resilience in the face of external changes.

- Identify diminishing returns, where thinly spread investments are resulting in growing complexity with lower output.

- Align investments to constantly assess whether existing systems are scalable or affordable in the long term.

DISCUSSION POINT: Simplify to minimize
the costs of complexity and maximize
leveraged returns

Discuss these five questions with your team and
simplify your business right away:

1. How can you simplify products to stay well
   above the nuisance threshold of users and build
   good habits?

2. How can you increase adaptability by
   abandoning blueprint-based, committee-
   consensus decision-making in true uncertainty?

3. What overhead tasks and processes can you
   completely discard or combine and modularize
   or automate?

4. How can you radically rethink neutral processes
   through simplification and redesign by
   refactoring past incremental fixes to increase
   antifragility?

5. How can you modularize complexity, to
   standardize and simplify, and to ensure
   adaptability while scaling to avoid collapse from
   the growing costs of complexity?

Simplified growth machines

The following two case studies illustrate how large
companies were built through organic growth and a
series of successful acquisitions by ensuring simplified,
standardized alignment and execution to leveraged

opportunities, thereby keeping the cost of complexity under control to scale and maximize returns.

CASE STUDY: Simplifying financial ecosystems – How Hypoport became a digital behemoth in credit, real estate, and insurance

Would you, as a twenty-five-year-old, take a personal loan of more than €7.5 million to lead a management buyback of the company you worked in?

Would you then, as CEO, be able to make the business compound at double-digit growth over a quarter century?

That's exactly what Ronald Slabke did when, along with his former manager, he bought back Dr Klein and created Hypoport. Slabke, right after his studies, had initially joined the small, family-owned B2C mortgage broker Dr Klein, where he soon became the assistant to the CEO. He quickly proved that he was good with money, says Slabke in the OMR podcast.[57] So good, that, at the age of twenty-five, he took out a personal loan for 15 million Deutschmark (more than €7.5 million today) and bought back the company after a sale. This encapsulates the birth of Hypoport and the legend of Ronald Slabke.

Summary

Hypoport, under the visionary leadership of Slabke, has since the late 1990s transformed Germany's financial services landscape. This has been achieved via the standardization and consolidation of digital processes into scalable processes across the credit, real estate, and insurance sectors. Leveraging a modular, platform-based approach, Hypoport's subsidiaries like Europace, Dr Klein, and Smart InsurTech have scaled by keeping complexity under control. By 2023 Hypoport's platforms facilitated about €100 billion in transactions annually, growing its revenues to €500 million, with an average year-over-year growth rate of 15%. This case study examines how Hypoport's simplified digital-first strategy propelled its rise and the role of key leaders like Slabke in driving innovation and efficiency.

Context

By the turn of the millennium, Germany's financial services sector was ripe for disruption. It was plagued by fragmented processes, high transaction costs, and siloed operations among banks, brokers, and insurers. Hypoport identified an opportunity to address these inefficiencies by building digital platforms that interconnected stakeholders, streamlined operations, and reduced costs. The vision was to create a financial ecosystem where credit, real estate, and insurance services could operate seamlessly through simplified, user-friendly, and standardized APIs and digital processes.

Challenges

Hypoport faced significant challenges:

- **Fragmented market:** The financial services sector operates in silos, with brokers, banks, and insurers not collaborating on a unified infrastructure to share data and streamline transactions.

- **Resistance to change:** Many traditional financial institutions were slow to adopt digital solutions due to legacy investments and risk aversion.

To become a dominant player, Hypoport needed to overcome these hurdles by creating scalable, standardized platforms that could address the entire value chain across multiple industries. The way Hypoport built APIs, to modularize complexity and provide flexibility and ease of use to customers and stakeholders, is very similar to the way Amazon built technology that it eventually monetized as Amazon Web Services, which resulted in the birth of the cloud.

Methodology

Hypoport's approach centered on building interconnected, modular platforms and APIs that standardized processes:

1. **Leadership and vision**

   - Slabke, CEO since 2002, was instrumental in driving the company's platform-first approach. His emphasis on scalability and modular design allowed Hypoport's platforms to evolve with market demands.

2. **Platform development**

   - **Europace**, Hypoport's flagship credit platform, facilitates seamless interactions between banks, brokers, and customers through APIs. By digitizing the end-to-end mortgage process, Europace became the largest credit marketplace in Germany, handling billions of euros in transactions annually.

   - **Smart InsurTech** standardized and automated insurance policy management, connecting insurers, brokers, and customers through a unified platform.

3. **Simplification and standardization**
   - APIs, data formats, and transaction protocols were standardized across platforms to enable interoperability.
   - Automated workflows were implemented for processes like credit scoring, policy issuance, and portfolio management.

4. **Customer-centric approach**
   - Platforms were designed with user-friendly interfaces and modular APIs to enhance accessibility for brokers and end customers.
   - Data-driven models were integrated to provide personalized recommendations and optimize decision-making for users.

Outcomes

Hypoport's approach yielded remarkable results over a decade and a half after its listing in 2007.

- **Revenue growth:** Annual revenues increased 11×, from €40 million in 1998 to €455 million by 2022.[58]

- **High profitability:** Annual gross profits increased 8×, from €31 million in 1998 to €260 million by 2022.[59]

- **Market share:** Market share grew to about one-third of total loan volume in Germany.

- **Acquisitions and network:** A decentralized network of twenty-five organically grown and inorganically acquired and integrated companies was created. This empowered Hypoport to serve a wide range of customers and stakeholders across financial services.

Key takeaways

1. **Leadership vision:** Slabke's foresight in prioritizing scalability and standardization was instrumental in Hypoport's rise. His leadership exemplifies the importance of aligning technology investments with long-term strategic goals.

2. **Standardization driving efficiency:** Unified data formats and processes reduced complexity and costs, enabling Hypoport to scale its operations while maintaining quality.

3. **The power of platforms:** Hypoport's success highlights the potential of platform-based business models to disrupt traditional industries. By creating interconnected ecosystems, companies can unlock value by driving liquidity, efficiency, and scalability.

4. **Partnership and network effects:** Hypoport's ability to partner with industry stakeholders ensured widespread adoption of its platforms. Building trust and fostering collaboration are critical for driving systemic change.

5. **Customer-centric design:** By prioritizing user experience, Hypoport ensured its platforms were not only efficient but also accessible and intuitive, driving high levels of adoption.

Conclusion

Hypoport's transformation – from its origins as a traditional B2C brick-and-mortar mortgage broking family business into a digital data-driven powerhouse – demonstrates the transformative potential of technology and effective leadership in legacy industries.

By standardizing and consolidating processes across credit, real estate, and insurance, the company built scalable platforms that delivered unparalleled value to stakeholders.

Under the leadership of Ronald Slabke, Hypoport not only disrupted traditional financial services but also set a new benchmark for digital and data-driven value creation. Hypoport has never paid out a dividend since listing on the public markets. Slabke has compounded double-digit growth for almost a quarter century (1998–2022) by reinvesting profits into growth. Very few companies in Germany have grown at such a high rate over such a long period.

Many companies slow down or collapse when they try to grow inorganically. The opposite applies to Hypoport, with its disciplined playbook or simplification, standardization, and decentralized execution. The company continues to compound growth, and its journey so far offers invaluable lessons for businesses seeking to reinvent themselves and thrive in the digital data-driven age.

CASE STUDY: Simplified compounding value creation playbook – How Brad Jacobs mastered the art of roll-ups and spin-outs

In 1979, at the age of twenty-three and shortly after dropping out of Brown University, Brad Jacobs cofounded Amerex Oil Associates. He'd decided to try his hand at oil brokerage. He had no existing industry contacts or relationships, but with his bold, first-principles entrepreneurial ingenuity, Jacobs hit his first home run.

Jacobs cold-called various executives at major oil companies, telling them he had barrels of oil to buy and sell. Once he identified a need from one party, he would cold-call until he found another company willing to fulfill the need, in effect brokering a deal created by crystalizing the hidden potential in the intransparent oil markets of the time. This approach required astute negotiation skills and the ability to build trust quickly in a high-stakes industry.

Thanks to Jacobs' quintessential chutzpah, Amerex grew rapidly, opening offices in Houston, London, Tokyo, and New Jersey. By the time Jacobs sold the business in 1983, Amerex had grown to a USD 4.7 billion annual brokerage volume and was recognized as one of the world's largest oil brokerage firms. This legendary first success laid the foundation for Jacobs' subsequent ventures, including his work in legacy, not popularly discussed industries like waste management, logistics, and equipment rental.[60]

Summary

Brad Jacobs, a seasoned serial entrepreneur, consolidated and revolutionized fragmented legacy industries through strategic use of roll-ups and consolidation. As founder and executive leader of XPO Logistics, Jacobs intelligently acquired then ruthlessly simplified and standardized processes and streamlined operations to scale the company into a USD 19 billion global logistics leader. Later he spun out companies like GXO Logistics, the largest pure-play contract logistics provider; and RXO, a leading freight brokerage. By consolidating technology, unifying operations, and focusing on rational, data-driven decision-making, Jacobs delivered exponential growth, operational excellence, and shareholder value.

This case study explores Jacobs' successful playbook of multiple decades and iterations, emphasizing the pivotal role of leadership and disciplined execution in reshaping the traditional legacy logistics industry. For more on Brad Jacobs' remarkable life and ideas, read his book *How to Make a Few Billion Dollars*.[61]

Context

Brad Jacobs began his career consolidating and reshaping legacy non-trendy industries, like waste management and equipment rentals, before turning to logistics in 2011 with the acquisition of XPO Logistics. At the time, XPO was a regional player with an annual revenue of just USD 175 million. Jacobs identified a fragmented logistics industry ripe for consolidation and growth through technological standardization and customer-centricity.

By 2021 XPO had grown into one of the world's largest logistics firms, supporting industries ranging from retail to e-commerce.[62] Jacobs then leveraged the potential to unlock even greater value through specialization, leading to spin-offs like GXO Logistics (contract logistics) and RXO (freight brokerage). These moves positioned each company to focus on core competencies, while maintaining robust growth trajectories.

Challenges

Jacobs faced several daunting challenges as he sought to reshape the legacy logistics sector:

- **Fragmented landscape:** The logistics and supply chain industries were composed of small, regional players with disparate systems and inconsistent service levels, leading to overall poor customer experience and satisfaction.

- **Operational complexity:** Dozens of acquisitions were integrated, through simplification and standardization of all technologies, workflows, processes, and company values and cultures.

- **Capital allocation:** Scaling acquisitions while maintaining profitability required a disciplined financial strategy.

Methodology

Jacobs employed a multipronged strategy to address these challenges:

1. **Strategic acquisitions**

   - Jacobs acquired more than seventeen companies between 2011 and 2015, including Con-way[63] and Norbert Dentressangle,[64] to build scale and market presence across North America and Europe.

   - He listened to the ideas and input for improving the acquired companies from all their employees, thereby galvanizing the employees by making them feel heard and enabling the best ideas to gain traction.

   - He spoke extensively with the customers of the newly acquired companies to understand their frustration, challenges, and needs, while committing to provide them an even better customer experience.

2. **Standardization and simplification**

   - Disparate systems were migrated into a simplified standard, enabling streamlined data analytics, and seamless process standardization and integration.

- Processes such as pricing, contract negotiation, and warehouse management were standardized to reduce inefficiencies and improve customer experience through economies of scale.

3. **Data-driven leverage**

- Jacobs invested heavily in proprietary software and data-driven automation, including machine learning for demand forecasting, inventory optimization, and robotics for warehouse operations.

- A revenue-generating digital freight marketplace was built to improve carrier efficiency and reduce costs.

4. **Spin-out strategy**

- In 2021 GXO Logistics was spun off to focus on contract logistics, capitalizing on the e-commerce boom.

- In 2022 RXO was created as a pure-play freight brokerage, leveraging digital tools to match carriers with shippers more efficiently.

5. **Leadership and alignment**

- A high-performance culture was fostered, focusing on delighting customers, true ownership through performance-based incentives, and extreme accountability.

- Top-tier talent was recruited to lead the spin-offs in an empowered, incentivized, and aligned manner.

Outcomes

Brad Jacobs' quintessential strategies and execution produced phenomenal results:

- **Revenue growth**
  - XPO Logistics grew revenues from USD 175 million in 2011 to USD 7.7 billion by 2022.[65]
  - GXO reported annual revenues exceeding USD 8 billion in its first year of operations.
- **Market leadership**
  - GXO became the world's largest contract logistics provider, serving top-tier clients such as Nike and Apple.[66]
  - RXO emerged as a leading freight brokerage firm, with advanced digital platforms driving efficiency.
- **Relentless value creation**
  - Processes and data-driven decision-making were simplified and standardized, improving service quality and reliability while reducing costs.
  - Significant synergies were achieved across acquisitions, through leverage, alignment, simplification, optimization, and relentless growth, generating many billions in shareholder value.
  - Jacobs' leadership and disciplined capital allocation resulted in substantial returns for investors, with XPO stock delivering returns of more than 1,000% during his tenure.

Key takeaways

1. **Visionary leadership is critical**
    -   Jacobs' ability to see opportunities in fragmented markets and execute a disciplined strategy was key to his success.
    -   Gedankenexperimenten and rigorous first principles thinking and execution, with a maverick flair, provide a winning playbook.

2. **Technology is a game-changer**
    -   Investing in proprietary technology and automation integrated into core processes leads to efficiency gains and differentiated services.

3. **Focus drives value**
    -   Spinning off GXO and RXO allowed each entity to focus on its core strengths, enhancing operational performance and market positioning.
    -   A relentless focus on ROI and strategic alignment, to achieve economies of scale without letting the cost of complexity get out of control, ensured that acquisitions and spin-offs drove long-term growth.

4. **Culture and talent matter**
    -   A culture of true ownership can be built through aligning compensation and incentives to performance, extreme accountability, and rigor in decision-making, while attracting smart and ambitious mavericks to lead businesses.

Conclusion

Brad Jacobs' playbook for mergers, acquisitions, and spin-offs demonstrates the power of data-driven leverage, alignment, simplification, optimization, and growth in reinventing fragmented legacy industries. By leveraging digital, data-driven value creation, disciplined execution, and visionary leadership, Jacobs created a logistics empire that continues to redefine industry standards.[67]

As GXO, RXO, and XPO continue to evolve, their trajectories offer valuable lessons for legacy businesses seeking to thrive in complex, traditional markets. Jacobs' legendary track record is a testament to the impact of a clear bold vision and relentless focus on value creation for customers.

FIVE

Optimize

I n this chapter we will look at how you can optimize learning and impact with an empirically valid
model. This starts with identifying the type of environment you operate in.

Know your environment

In 1999 Dave Snowden developed the Cynefin
Framework to help decision-makers frame the context they are operating in.[68] *Cynefin* – the Welsh word
for habitat – defines five types of domains in which a
decision-maker could be operating by characterizing
how the person perceives the domain to make sense
of their behavior and that of others.

Here are the five Cynefin domains:

1. **Clear:** Known knowns, cause, and effect are clear and predictable.

2. **Complicated:** Known unknowns, causes, and effects exist but are harder to discern because there could be multiple right answers.

3. **Complex:** Unknown unknowns, causes, and effects exist but can only be understood in hindsight. There are no right answers, because solutions emerge through experimentation.

4. **Chaotic:** There is unclear cause and effect, and immediate action is required to stabilize the situation.

5. **Confusion:** Everything is unclear, including in which Cynefin domain the situation is.

According to Dave Snowden and his co-author Mary Boone, as knowledge increases, there is a drift from chaotic to complex to complicated to clear. Similarly, a drift in the opposite direction can take place as knowledge reduces. The objective should always be to increase knowledge to make the domain more optimizable.

A direct transition from clear to chaotic can take place if people try to force situations to become clear by glossing over empirical realities through oversimplification.

One example of this is how repeated, oversimplified cost-cutting measures at Boeing led to two crashes of the Boeing 737 MAX, leading to a grounding of the fleets, regulatory investigations, and massive reputational damage to the Boeing brand.[69] Another reason for a direct transition from clear to chaotic could be due to sudden unforeseen disruptions. An obvious example of this is the effect of the Covid pandemic on live in-person events. Another less sudden but equally far-reaching example is the change from the industrial to the digital, data-driven value creation paradigm.

This is why having an empirically valid worldview, with a rigorous understanding of the domain and environment you are operating in, is critical to intelligent decision-making to optimize outcomes. Before even starting to think about a decision, ask yourself which Cynefin domain you are in. To know your environment:

- **Report:** Analyze the past to uncover hypotheses and dynamics.

- **Validate:** Experiment and test empirically.

- **React:** Monitor in real time.

- **Anticipate:** Estimate future states.

A well-defined problem

Every paradigm for decision-making and execution has an underlying worldview that needs to be coherent for any value to be created. In physics you cannot believe that the world is Newtonian, disregard the theory of relativity, and then expect to develop precise GPS technology. Similarly, you cannot believe that the world is Newtonian, disregard quantum mechanics, and then want to build a modern mobile phone. Similarly, in chemistry you can't believe that the world is made up of the five elements (earth, water, air, fire, ether) and then insist on using Mendeleev's periodic table and the structure of atoms.

In financial markets you can't believe in complete market efficiency and then raise money for an actively managed fund. That is contradictory and incoherent.

In business you can't use the principles of agriculture to be successful in the industrial age of machines, factories, and mass production. Similarly, you cannot apply the paradigm of manufacturing physical goods to building and scaling a software company.

Empirically valid model

For success in true uncertainty, the focus has to be on empirically valid rational thinking that optimizes decision-making to achieve the best possible outcome at each iteration. This involves understanding the environment you are operating in, for example by using the Cynefin Framework as guidance, to rigorously formulate and pose the problem such that it is valid and mathematically optimizable.

An effective strategy works when you have abstracted execution to a point where you have a well-defined problem, with an empirically valid set of variables and trade-offs. By developing a quantitative empirically valid abstraction, you can transform complex ambiguous environments into problems that are clear and structured, and that have actionable impactful outcomes. This allows you to make high-conviction decisions for capital allocation. In this sense, strategy is not a theoretical framework. It is a clear, empirically valid, actionable, and practical tool for maximizing business impact.

Without this empirically valid mathematical formulation, an ill-posed unclear problem invariably involves a sub-optimal solution, arrived at through unnecessary randomization and arbitrariness in decision-making.

As an example of what this means, let's go back to the probability-matching World War II US Air Force pilots we spoke about at the start of the chapter on leverage. We already discussed why probability matching is not an optimal strategy, and it did not maximize the pilots' probability of survival. Let's build an empirically valid mathematical abstraction of their problem to illustrate the value of empirically valid well-defined mathematical abstractions. The decision the pilots had to make was to pick either a flak jacket or a parachute before each flight. The probability of getting shot at was significantly higher than the entire aircraft being shot down.

For the sake of this example, let's say the probability of the flak jacket saving the pilot's life was 70%, and the probability of the parachute saving the pilot's life was 30%. You can replace this whole setting with a casino slot machine that has two arms, one arm representing the flak jacket and another arm representing the parachute. In this case, since the US Air Force had collected data across all sorties, they already identified which slot machine arm had the best payoff.

Now suppose you were among the first set of pilots flying sorties, then this abstraction of the decision problem would allow you to learn the optimal strategy very quickly. The reason is that this well-defined problem allows you to make valid assumptions on the underlying distribution of the two arms of the slot machine, namely that they are independent (every sortie is a new mission with new information) and identically distributed (the enemy's ability to shoot down aircraft doesn't vary drastically over time).

In reinforcement learning this is called a *stochastic bandit*. That's because slot machine abstractions are called *multi-armed bandit problems*, and because the adjective *stochastic* means the underlying probability distribution of each arm is independent and identically distributed. Due to these mathematical constraints on the underlying distribution of their arms, stochastic bandits can be optimized for with a logarithmic regret bound. In short, after a few iterations, you can quickly learn which arm has the best payoff. In the pilot example, the fact is that the flak jacket is much better than the parachute. Broadly, the optimal learning algorithm in this case involves choosing the arm with the best payoff – the flak jacket almost all the time – and infrequently checking the other arm, to ensure the patterns in the observations so far remain valid.

Now suppose we did not take the pains to define an empirically valid model that captures the regularity and known structures of the environment the pilots are operating in. What if we made no assumptions on the probability distributions of the two arms?

We would then be left with what is called an *adversarial bandit* – essentially, a multi-armed bandit with no assumptions made on the underlying distribution of the arms. Mathematically speaking, this is the strongest generalization of the multi-armed bandit problem. The fewer the assumptions made, the more general the problem, and the less optimal the mathematical solution.

Randomization in decision-making is a critical component in any strategy in an adversarial setting where the environment is unknown and hence no assumptions can be made on regularity. Seen through this lens, the probability matching of the pilots seems less absurd. Given that the pilots didn't use a well-defined empirically valid model of the world to make their decisions, they chose to randomize their choices. For most of our history as a species, we haven't had the resources to extensively model and compute to understand our environment and to control it. Aggressive randomization allowed us to survive.

Satisficing was our survival strategy for a low-energy, low-compute, dangerous world. None of these assumptions about our context hold anymore, because we have large amounts of cheap compute available to use today, and we can also collect, curate, model, and analyze data with relative ease. Our ability to build a layer of abstraction – an empirically valid well-defined mathematical problem – is now the key to unlocking optimal solutions by leveraging the vast data and computing at our disposal. Satisficing is no longer a useful survival strategy, because there are some humans who have stopped satisficing by building empirically valid, well-defined mathematical models of the world, by leveraging data and computing to act more rationally. This makes these humans' orders of magnitude more effective than others. Satisficing is now no longer an evolutionarily useful survival strategy.

How can I, in this book, help you arrive at a well-defined problem, without knowing your environment or the problem you are trying to solve?

In practice, most models involve some sort of forecasting, combined with optimization. Defining general principles by making statements, however, adds constraints and reduces the solution space, and hence increases the probability that the optimum solution is no longer in the constrained solution space. That is why I am unable to provide you with general principles without knowing the exact environment and type of problem you are looking to optimize and solve.

On the other hand, asking questions leads to new dimensions or growing the solution space, thereby adding potentially even better optima to the expanded solution space. With this objective in mind, let me share with you a list of questions that have helped me formulate well-defined problems across varying types of environments:

Defining the objective

1. What is the purpose of the model?

2. How will the success of the model be measured?

3. How can the success of the model be further leveraged?

4. What are the consequences of model failure?

5. What characterizes the interaction between the model and humans?

Understanding the environment

1. What are the key variables and components of the environment?

2. What are the relationships and interactions between these variables?

3. What are the boundaries of the environment?

4. What measurable quantities represent the components and their interactions?

5. What data is available or required to describe the environment and variables?

Setting characteristics and constraints

1. What constraints or rules govern the environment?

2. What noise or irreducible uncertainty exists in the environment?

3. How does the environment evolve over time or under changing conditions?

4. Are there any known feedback loops in the environment?

5. Are there emergent behaviors like, for example, network effects?

Starting validation and refinement

1. What assumptions can be empirically validated?

2. How can regularity be maximized?

3. What criteria will determine if the model is valid?

4. What are the limitations of the model?

5. What iterative processes will refine the model?

Using the model

1. How will the outputs of the model be used?

2. How will the model's findings be used or communicated?

3. What are the key uncertainties or gaps in understanding?

4. How does this model integrate with existing knowledge or systems?

5. How can human–model interaction be leveraged further?

Don't just forecast but also optimize the decision

Businesses tend to spend so much time, resources, and effort in building models for forecasting revenue, units sold, customer churn, and more. Usually, it is the finance function that pushes hardest for data-driven forecasts. At their core, forecasts help reduce uncertainty, which allows you to act proactively to shape the future. Forecasting is increasingly done by data-driven algorithms, but unfortunately, acting on those forecasts continues to remain solely in the purview of humans. Mundane decisions are therefore not optimized to realize the full potential of algorithmic decision-making outcomes at scale.

There are primarily three types of forecasts used by businesses:

1. Financial planning forecasts

2. Resource allocation forecasts

3. Operational efficiency forecasts

Given that financial planning has a one-off value, it falls in the overhead category of the Data Impact LNO Framework for data-driven value creation. Resource allocation and operational efficiency have relatively constant returns over time and are thus neutral, but fast-growing opportunities would also be in the leverage category. Since financial planning is usually a critical finance job, in close collaboration with the executive team, let us quickly go through an effective, resource- and capital-efficient method to complete data-driven financial planning.

Forecasting is a wicked problem. Define a clear benchmark you want to beat. Almost always, a previously used forecasting method or a weighted rolling average gives a good baseline. You will be surprised how hard weighted rolling averages are to beat, especially for data with cancellation or averaging effects like revenue forecasting. Embrace the irreducible uncertainty of the world – accept that your forecast will always be different from the actual values. Timebox efforts to avoid going down the rabbit hole intrinsic to wicked problems. Focus the algorithms on the power laws to intelligently automate the highest volume of granular decisions; for example, focus on about 80% of the customers or about 80% of the revenue. Let the humans focus on interpreting and acting on the outliers and one-off instances. Or, when possible, define robust heuristics to deal with the outliers.

Benchmarking forecast quality

Forecast value added (FVA) is a metric that quantifies the improvement in forecast accuracy achieved by each component or step in a multistep forecasting process.[70] It quantifies which activities improve the quality of predictions, and which introduce errors or add no value. The advantage of FVA is that it helps ensure that any resources invested in the forecasting process – from compute resources to the time and energy of employees and executives – are making the forecast better.

Implementing FVA is straightforward and very important, to prevent forecasting efforts from getting buried in the bottomless pit of wicked problems. The implementation process runs as follows:

1. Take your best algorithmic forecast, based on the approach defined above, and use it as a baseline forecast for FVA.

2. Measure the accuracy of this baseline forecast against the accuracy of forecasts modified by humans in different steps or processes over time.

3. Analyze whether each stage led to a worsening or improvement in accuracy.

4. Remove steps in the process that degrade the forecast quality or that don't improve it.

5. Focus your resources exclusively on activities that add measurable value. The seniority of the person asking to change the forecast is irrelevant; only the value addition to the forecast accuracy matters.

Optimizing decisions

For resource allocation and operational efficiency, the major problem is that most people obsess about the accuracy of forecasts and then don't bother optimizing decisions or algorithmically automating the high volume of tedious decisions to create massive value at scale.

OPTIMIZE

It doesn't matter if rain is forecast for tomorrow if you still go out without an umbrella. Similarly, it doesn't matter how good your demand forecast is if you don't use it to optimize your inventory decisions and outcomes.

Massive value creation is unlocked when algorithms not only do the forecasting but also integrate forecasting with optimized and automated decision-making of the high-volume or high-frequency tedious decisions. Why would you make humans do an algorithm's job?

Humans primarily use point forecasts to grapple with the future, ie exact values for a variable in the future. For example, people want to know how many units of a product will sell in the next week. There are multiple reasons for this, including the cognitive load of processing vast amounts of granular information, discomfort with uncertainty, a bias towards deterministic interpretations, inadequate common decision-making frameworks, and the complexity of conveying probabilistic information. Ultimately, data-driven algorithms are about forcing us as humans to challenge our behavioral biases and irrationality, to improve the quality of our rational decision-making.

Probabilistic forecasts, combined with optimization, allow for the construction of leveraged asymmetric bets – where with heads you win big and tails you don't lose much. This approach allows taking neutral

151

tasks like resource allocation and operational efficiency and leveraging them in a data-driven manner to squeeze out growing payoffs that can compound over time to drive phenomenal growth. This approach of building leveraged asymmetric bets is commonplace and mainstream among traders in the financial markets, but it is still very rare as a decision-making approach among legacy businesses.

To illustrate this point, let's look first at a simple example from the financial markets.

Point forecast scenario: A trader gets a point forecast that a stock's price will increase by 10% the next day. Based on this single estimate, the trader decides to buy a huge quantity of the stock, assuming it's a strong, certain opportunity for profit.

Probabilistic forecast scenario: The trader receives a probabilistic forecast showing the following outcomes:

- 50% chance the stock will increase in price by about 10%

- 30% chance the stock will remain flat with a 0% change in price

- 20% chance the stock will decrease in price by about 5%

With this detailed distribution of future outcomes, the trader can size the amount of stock purchased to reflect the risk of loss (eg, a 20% chance of a 5% drop). They could also hedge their position with options or diversify their investment to manage the downside risk better. If the trader is managing a larger portfolio, then the probabilities can be incorporated as part of a wider portfolio strategy that accounts for both risk and return.

The outcome is that the probabilistic forecast allows the trader to balance risk and reward effectively, potentially avoiding significant losses or overexposure to a single stock. This forecast has allowed the trader to build a leveraged asymmetric bet. By accounting for the range of possible outcomes and their probabilities, the trader achieves highly leveraged risk-adjusted returns that are far superior to the simplistic point forecast and naïve decision to go long. A point forecast provides a misleading sense of certainty, increasing the risk of a poorly calibrated decision.

Mapping either scenario to the resource allocation and operational efficiency decisions made by a manufacturer, supplier, wholesaler, or retailer is very straightforward.

Point forecast scenario: A retail store gets a point forecast for sales of 100 units of a product for the upcoming week. The store manager decides to stock exactly 100 units.

Probabilistic forecast scenario: Instead of a point forecast represented by a single number for the units of a product sold the upcoming week, a probabilistic forecast provides a range of demand scenarios with probabilities:

- 80% chance demand will be 90–110 units

- 10% chance demand will be below 90 units

- 10% chance demand will exceed 110 units

The manager can now leverage this information to optimize the decision by balancing stockout risks and holding costs. For example, if the cost of stockouts is higher than the cost of excess inventory, the manager might stock 110 units to cover the ninetieth percentile of demand. Alternatively, if holding costs are very high, the manager can compute the risk-adjusted optimal level of inventory to keep, to maximize returns.

The outcome in the case of the point forecast is that if the demand is higher than 100 (eg, 120 units), the store loses sales due to stockouts. If demand is lower than 100 (eg, 80 units), the store incurs holding costs for the excess inventory. By considering the nuanced probabilistic forecast, the manager can optimize the inventory decision to minimize total costs (stockout + holding). This approach results in better financial outcomes than a reliance on the point forecast alone, which glosses over the irreducible uncertainty and does not leverage the power of data-driven algorithms.

For a more detailed deep dive into how leading European electronics and appliances retailer Worten worked together with Lokad to bring to life Lokad founder and CEO Joannès Vermorel's vision of the quantitative supply chain, read the first case study below.[71]

DISCUSSION POINT: Optimize decisions for value creation

Discuss these five questions with your team to optimize your business right away:

1. How can you identify the type of environment you operate in to design your decision-making and learning approach?

2. What is an empirically valid abstraction that is mathematically optimizable for the environment you operate in?

3. How can you optimize the impact of your decisions by taking into account the full distribution of outcomes?

4. Which irreducible uncertainties of the environment should you embrace to prevent oversimplification?

5. How can you extract maximum regularity from your environment to minimize randomization in decision-making?

Optimizing with a vision

The first of the case studies below illustrates how one legacy business implemented the quantitative supply chain, an empirically valid optimized model of logistics. The second shows how a decade-old business in a legacy sector built an optimized, data-driven, highly profitable value proposition on top of its legacy operations.

CASE STUDY: The quantitative supply chain – How Worten and Lokad built a quantitative supply chain designed for the twenty-first century

Note: This case study has been adapted and reproduced from the one created by Lokad and with full permission from Lokad.[72]

Worten is a leading Portuguese electronics and appliance retailer, operating more than 300 stores and a robust online platform, with extensive product selections. Worten's omnichannel operations are made even more difficult, given the sheer volume of products in its offering – more than 40,000 stock keeping units (SKUs). Frustrated by the limitations of mainstream approaches, Worten decided it needed a paradigm shift and thus engaged Lokad to help start the retailer's quantitative supply chain revolution.

Summary

In the early 2020s Worten found itself at a supply chain crossroads. It did not want to rest on its laurels, yet evolving was proving difficult. Bruno Saraiva, Worten's head of stock and space management, believed the problem stemmed from reliance on old-school supply chain approaches – ideas that were simply incapable of meeting the complexity and uncertainty of Worten's supply chain operations. This realization presented Worten with significant philosophical, technological, and operational challenges.

Inventory decisions were often based on a combination of Excel spreadsheets and manual intervention – an approach that overlooked the complexity of Worten's supply chain needs. This led Saraiva and his team to reflect on the true nature of the problem they were trying to solve. Rather than ignoring the uncertainty of future demand – a common feature of classic time-series forecasting – Worten decided they needed to actively model it. That meant rethinking its inventory decisions probabilistically.

In turn, this philosophical and mathematical realization presented significant technological and operational challenges. Worten wanted a software solution that could handle the combinatorial complexity of decision-making for the giant's omnichannel retail network. Moreover, these decisions needed to account for Worten's enormous array of constraints, drivers, and customer promises. Operationally, Worten did not want to be stuck in a never-ending software implementation limbo where the costs and lead times grow year-on-year. This is unfortunately quite common in enterprise software upgrades or migrations.

According to Saraiva, "Through the external events I was attending, I could feel that a new way of managing and optimizing inventory was emerging. The challenges

157

Covid brought to our supply chain reinforced my conviction that it was time to move out of our comfort zone and keep learning – potentially revolutionizing our inventory management decision-making. We thus decided to manage our legacy systems upgrade as an opportunity to do so, rather than just a risk on a purely technical transition."

Challenges

Traditionally, Worten's inventory management relied on deterministic forecasts and manual processes, which proved insufficient for managing the enormous variety of products and distribution channels. Worten also utilized manual decision-making over advanced automation. This made quick restocking and maintaining high product availability much more difficult, which naturally impacted customer satisfaction.

To properly grasp the scope of Worten's supply chain complexity, one must also bear in mind the sheer scale of Worten's operations:

- 40,000+ SKUs in catalog
- 300+ stores
- >€1 billion turnover
- Physical and online retail
- At-home and in-store delivery for customers, eg, ordering online or in Store A, then receiving the product in Store A (at that time or later), in Store B, or at home

Add to this the steep expectations Worten sets for itself in terms of customer service: customers should be able to buy/preorder an item even if it is currently out of stock in a given store. If an item is out of stock in Store A, a customer should still be able to buy it and have it transferred to Store A from the nearest available store/warehouse. This level of retail flexibility and dependability means stockouts and delays are critical pain points.

In short, Worten needed a solution that could:

- Manage its complex supply chain network of 300+ stores, 40,000+ SKUs, and 1,000+ suppliers
- Balance its inventory across an omnichannel retail environment
- Generate its necessary store replenishment and purchasing decisions daily, and *under real-world constraints* (store space limitations, warehouse capacity, etc)

Methodology

- Worten collaborated with Lokad to overhaul and revolutionize their supply chain. An initial step in this journey was transitioning away from Worten's previous deterministic approach to forecasting (eg, demand). Deterministic in this context means predicting a single value based on the assumption that the future (eg, the number of units customers will buy next week) can be known.

This deterministic approach is flawed as it ignores the full range of possible future values (eg, customers could buy 1 unit, 2 units, 3 units, or even 0 units). It also means that a company cannot estimate and compare the financial rewards of different scenarios, such as the economic return of selling 7 units versus 10 units versus only 1 unit. In reality, your chances of selling 3 units versus 4 units might be very similar, but the economic returns could be significantly different (once you consider your constraints and drivers, eg, minimum order quantity [MOQ] and lot multipliers).

For this reason, Lokad uses probabilistic forecasting as it provides the scenario simulation that companies like Worten need to make better supply chain decisions. Importantly, Lokad applies probabilistic forecasting to all relevant sources of uncertainty, including customer demand, supplier lead times, supplier service level, returns, etc.

Lokad's supply chain scientists (SCS) – the people who design and execute the decision-making algorithms – then combined the probabilistic forecasts with advanced stochastic optimization techniques to simplify Worten's supply chain decision-making processes.

This allowed Lokad's SCS team to:

- Forecast the totality of Worten's demand scenarios for 40,000+ SKUs
- Generate 45,000+ inventory decisions daily
- Automate decision-making across multiple warehouses, an online platform, and 300+ stores across several regions (Portugal, Canary Islands, Azores, Madeira)
- Optimize (financially) Worten's reorder and allocation logic (RAL)
- Replace spreadsheets with intuitive dashboards to monitor supply chain health

Outcomes

The success of Worten's collaboration with Lokad is measured across several criteria and KPIs, including change management, inventory performance, and customer satisfaction:

- Successful end user buy-in and high user adoption of Lokad's solution and philosophy, saving dozens of working hours per user per week (50+ people) – no more Excel and manual overrides
- 17.8% reduction in stockouts, resulting in an additional 0.78% generated revenue and a 0.63% increase in front-office margin for the retail business
- 7.8% reduction of overall stock value held in stores
- Improved free cash flow by buying at the right time and improving stock rotations by several percentage points
- Double-digit reduction of inventory net of facing (eg, display and test units) at stores, reducing cash flow needed to keep the retail business running
- 5% improvement to net promoter score (NPS), with Worten at the end of 2024 boasting a 42.1% NPS, compared with 37% in 2023

Key takeaways

Lokad introduced a new perspective and approach through its probabilistic forecasting, enabling Worten to evaluate the full range of possible future outcomes. Instead of working with a single predicted value, Worten at the end of 2024 employs scenario-based simulations, quantifying the financial return of stocking decisions across thousands of SKUs and hundreds of stores.

By combining these probabilistic forecasts with advanced stochastic optimization algorithms, Worten can systematically define inventory allocation, order timing, and replenishment decisions, to balance constraints such as warehouse capacity and store space limitations.

This advanced modeling directly translates into measurable gains. Worten achieved a 17.8% reduction in stockouts, which drove revenue growth and margin improvements, evidenced by a 0.78% revenue increase and a 0.63% rise in the front-office margin.

Simultaneously, this provided a 7.8% reduction in overall store stock levels as well as a double-digit reduction in inventory net of facing. This freed up cash flow and improved stock rotations by several percentage points. Worten also realized a 5% improvement to its NPS, at the end of 2024 boasting a 42.1% NPS compared with 37% in 2023.

Importantly, Worten transitioned away from spreadsheets and manual overrides, instead now using automation and intuitive dashboards that yield substantial time savings for 50+ employees. This enhanced operational efficiency enables staff to focus on strategic initiatives rather than manual tasks.

Conclusion

Worten's successful collaboration with Lokad sets the foundation for future growth. Of particular interest, Worten intends to expand its spare parts and maintenance services in Portugal. Given Lokad's extensive expertise in the automotive aftermarket and aerospace maintenance, repair, and operations (MRO) sectors, the partnership is well positioned to continue delivering substantial value.

Lokad's quantitative supply chain vision allows companies to leverage their supply chain to optimize revenue and margins, using a financially adjusted perspective. This leveraged, aligned, simplified, and optimized vision of the world allows companies to convert their supply chain from a cost center to an engine of growth.

CASE STUDY: Monetizing grocery delivery
and demand – How Instacart built a profitable
advertising powerhouse

Instacart has emerged as a leader not only in grocery delivery but also in digital advertising. By leveraging its data-rich platform into an optimized advertising machine, Instacart unlocked a new revenue stream that propelled its profitability and scalability beyond its legacy grocery delivery business. Under the leadership of Fidji Simo, CEO since 2021, and key executives like Chief Revenue Officer Seth Dallaire, Instacart transitioned from a logistics-driven physical business to a digital, data-driven and physical business. By 2023 its ad business contributed an estimated USD 1 billion in revenue, with gross profit margins significantly exceeding those of its core delivery operations.[73] This case study examines how Instacart's innovative approach to advertising transformed the company into a highly profitable and rapidly growing data-driven powerhouse.

Summary

Founded in 2012, Instacart initially focused on delivering groceries from local stores directly to customers. By 2020 it had become a household name, particularly during the Covid pandemic, when demand for grocery delivery soared. However, its core delivery business faced challenges:

- **Low margins:** Traditional delivery operations yielded slim profit margins due to high operational costs.

- **Large competitors:** Competitors like Amazon Fresh and DoorDash were increasingly vying for market share.

- **Capital intensity:** Growth was constrained by scarcity of infrastructure and labor and required significant capital-intensive investments.

Instacart recognized that its treasure trove of shopper data – encompassing purchasing behavior, preferences, and patterns – could be monetized beyond delivery fees. The company began developing a robust advertising platform, shifting its revenue model and laying the foundation for highly profitable and diversified growth.

Challenges

Instacart's initial success in grocery delivery faced several challenges:

- **Profitability constraints:** Operating a delivery-based business at scale is capital-intensive, limiting profitability.

- **Increased competition:** Larger players like Amazon Fresh threatened to erode Instacart's market share and destroy profitability.

- **Untapped data potential:** Instacart had access to an immense dataset of proprietary granular shopper behaviors but was not leveraging it to generate revenue.

To address these challenges, Instacart needed to diversify its revenue streams and capitalize on its unique customer demand data, thanks to its dominant market position and well-liked brand.

Methodology

Instacart's advertising business was driven by four core elements:

1. **Decisive leadership**
   - CEO Fidji Simo, a former Facebook executive, brought an advertising tech-driven perspective to Instacart.
   - Seth Dallaire, with experience at Amazon and Walmart, spearheaded the monetization of Instacart's advertising assets, emphasizing efficiency and measurable ROI for brands.
   - COO Asha Sharma focused on integrating the advertising business with Instacart's logistics operations to ensure a seamless user experience.

2. **High-margin advertising platform**
   - "Instacart Ads" were introduced, allowing brands to promote products directly on the platform.
   - Proprietary first-party data was leveraged to offer hyper-targeted advertising based on real-time shopping behaviors.
   - Sponsored product placements and in-app promotions were implemented, seamlessly integrating ads into the user's shopping experience.

3. **Optimizing data utilization**
   - Advanced data-driven solutions were delivered, to provide advertisers with insights into customer preferences and purchase patterns.
   - Machine learning was used to optimize ad targeting and placements to maximize engagement and conversion rates.

4. **Creating value for brands**
   - Instacart partnered with leading consumer brands to deliver measurable advertising outcomes, driving incremental sales.

- Self-service ad tools were developed to make the platform accessible to businesses of all sizes.
- Non-grocery retailers were introduced to the platform, broadening the advertising opportunities and customer base.

Outcomes

Instacart's advertising strategy resulted in impressive success:

- **Diversified revenue growth:** Ad business revenue reached an estimated USD 1 billion by 2023, accounting for a growing share of overall revenue and, especially, profitability.[74]

- **Higher gross margins:** Advertising gross profit margins were reported to be around 70%, far exceeding the margins of the delivery business.

- **Customer engagement and relevance:** Sponsored products consistently achieved higher click-through and conversion rates due to precise targeting.

- **Emerging market leadership:** This established Instacart as a key emerging participant in the digital advertising market, competing with incumbent giants like Amazon and Google.

- **New business growth:** Revenue streams were diversified and reliance on legacy grocery business delivery fees were reduced, ensuring long-term viability and profitable growth.

Key takeaways

1. **Leadership drives impact:** Visionary executives like Fidji Simo and Seth Dallaire played critical roles in executing the highly leveraged data-driven pivot to advertising.

2. **Leverage legacy assets:** Instacart's success demonstrates the value of monetizing underutilized legacy assets such as first-party shopper data from the grocery delivery business.

3. **Customer-centric improvements:** By ensuring ads were relevant and not annoying, Instacart maintained a positive shopping experience for users while driving revenue.

4. **Self-serve scales well:** The self-service ad platform enabled rapid growth and scalability, providing value to businesses of all sizes, without increasing costs correspondingly driving up gross profit margins.

5. **Diversification is valuable:** Instacart's evolution to a diversified revenue model mitigated risks associated with scaling its legacy delivery business.

Conclusion

Instacart's evolution from a logistics-focused grocery delivery service to a highly profitable, data-driven advertising powerhouse highlights the massive value creation that results from leveraging the legacy business customer demand and proprietary data assets. Under the leadership of Fidji Simo, Seth Dallaire, and other exceptional executives, the company built a scalable, high-margin ad business that complemented its core legacy operations.

As Instacart continues to grow, its successful pivot and evolution offer valuable lessons for legacy businesses seeking to diversify revenue and optimize leveraged assets.

SIX

Grow

I n this chapter I will explain how shedding the scarcity mindset will help you to grow your legacy business. In a world of demand, maximum growth can be achieved by focusing on that demand and embracing an abundance mindset. As American author and speaker Marianne Williamson is reported to have said, key to abundance is addressing limited circumstances with unlimited thoughts.

Traditional supply-side disruption

According to Clayton Christensen's theory of disruption, a disruptive company is defined in a very specific manner.[75] A disruptor starts by offering a good enough product for low-value underserved customers. Disruption is thus a long process, and ironically, that is why incumbents often overlook disruptors. For example, when Netflix launched in 1997, it wasn't attractive to most of Blockbuster's existing customers, who wanted fast access to the latest movie releases. Netflix instead served a niche of movie aficionados who were not excited about the newest movies released but were early adopters of DVD players and online shopping.[76] That's probably why Blockbuster didn't bother. Had Netflix directly targeted Blockbuster's core customers and products, then Blockbuster would have probably immediately counterattacked with its full might.

Instead, Netflix grew on the sidelines over a whole decade, until it launched video streaming in 2007, suddenly offering a much better product than Blockbuster to Blockbuster's core customers. This illustrates how Netflix was a decade-long disruption happening in full sight. If Blockbuster had wanted to, it would have had a whole decade to act. Disruption theory by Clayton Christensen provides a clearly defined framework to deal with such phenomena.

However, not all new entrants are disruptors. Uber, for example, started by offering a better product to existing taxi industry customers and grew phenomenally. This kind of phenomenon is a massive danger not only to the survival of traditional incumbents, but it also takes place at a much faster pace than disruption. Clayton Christensen says, "According to disruption theory, Uber is an outlier, and we do not have a universal way to account for such atypical outcomes."[77]

Danger of new players that capture demand

What explains the phenomenon of new entrants decimating a traditional industry and capturing huge market share and profit margins?

New digital entrants, which are typically startups, succeed by capturing demand in legacy industries. They enter a market by providing a customer experience that is more convenient, cheaper, and trustworthy. For example, InsurTech, just like Uber, is all about delighting customers of traditional insurers with a better digital experience. In effect, InsurTech is capturing demand and serving it better, without necessarily changing supply – it is hard to reinvent insurance supply, and no company has radically reinvented insurance supply over the past decade. These new players emerged over the past decade by building a better digital experience to capture demand and plugging the traditional industrial offering in the background, effectively developing lucrative new distribution channels that own the customer's trust, convenience, and relationship.

The classic disruptors in your industry – ones that innovate on the supply side by providing a good product to your underserved customers – are well understood and covered by Clayton Christensen's work. There are well-documented and established playbooks for such situations. If you have a data-driven business, you can identify, monitor, and act against disruptors because disruption takes time, and traditional incumbents always have opportunities to counterattack.

What about the new players that quickly capture demand and risk the survival of your entire business?

These new players all have one thing in common: they focus on the demand side to grow rapidly. They leverage technology to provide a seamless user experience, build trust, and offer competitive prices. That is what FinTechs did in banking and insurance, and what marketplaces did to travel transportation and e-commerce. The supply-side disruptors are a challenge to your business, but supply-side disruptors take a long time to grow. If you're savvy, they also give you ample time to counterattack and win. The most existential danger to your business is new players who capture the demand side.

Abandon scarcity mindset and embrace abundance

The industrial paradigm, by its very nature, leads to a scarcity mindset by forcing you to think in terms of available resources:

- Raw material and physical input constraints
- Capital-intensive upfront investments

- Focus on supply costs and efficiency

- Cyclicity and regular scarring

- Competition and commoditization shift focus to cost control

In their book *Scarcity: Why having too little means so much*, behavioral economist Sendhil Mullainathan and behavioral scientist Eldar Shafir study the crippling effects of a scarcity mindset.[78] They argue that scarcity mindset results in tunneling, where our minds begin to obsess only on scarcity and hence ignore all the opportunities and abundance outside that scarcity tunnel. The authors also note that scarcity causes cognitive problem-solving capabilities to decline as it decreases mental bandwidth. This drop in cognitive abilities is shockingly large and measurable through lab and field experiments.

Tunneling, combined with decreased mental bandwidth, leads to a doom loop of firefighting one urgent task after another and completely ignoring the few high-leverage opportunities that matter. A scarcity mindset thus turns into a self-fulfilling prophecy of small thinking, leading at an increasing pace to ever smaller thinking. Activity becomes the barometer of progress instead of leveraged, aligned, simplified, and optimized outcomes that underpin growth. When the bean-counting monkey rides the terrified reptile, things end in catastrophe.

The digital, data-driven value-creation paradigm has low fixed costs and almost zero variable costs for replication and personalization. The solution, to overcome the scarcity mindset, is to focus on the abundance of customer demand to grow. Your customers are never satisfied and will have unmet dreams, wishes, and needs. Obsessing about fulfilling these with a leveraged, aligned, simplified, and optimized data-driven approach will allow you to continue compounding growth and delight your customers over decades.

For most consumer products, customers essentially care only for price, range, speed, and ease of use. All these factors are measurable, and your objective should be to leverage data-driven algorithms to improve them by at least 10× over the next years to compound growth at your legacy business over the next decade. The case studies in this book show you that this is possible. It has been successfully achieved by a whole range of differing businesses across a diverse array of industries.

As platform expert Sangeet Paul Choudary says, "Traditional supply chains need to manage the trade-off between utilization and availability. The ability to predict demand solves this trade-off and informs stocking and logistics."[79] By better understanding demand, you can better invest in supply-side assets. By leveraging the proprietary demand from your customers, using data-driven algorithms, you can optimize the supply side of your legacy business in ways that are impossible for others to replicate.

Your greatest moat is a 10× better product that your customers love. The more your customers love your product, the more they will get their friends to use it. The only scalable, sustainable, and profitable growth is driven by word of mouth. Once you forget resource constraints and scarcity, and instead obsess and iterate on customer demand – their unfulfilled hopes – you can uplift your purpose and grow in a world of opportunities and abundance.

Challenge of infrequent products

Legacy businesses often have core products that are infrequently purchased – residential real estate, cars, insurance policies, mortgages, household appliances, holiday travel, etc. These products face huge challenges in customer engagement and brand retention and thus struggle to grow in a world where user attention and time are constantly targeted by digital, data-driven experiences.

Research in psychology shows that humans do not retain information well unless memories are regularly stimulated.[80] With infrequent products, with long intervals between interactions, this results in customers forgetting their experiences of the product and brand. This in turn leads to reduced likelihood of repeat purchases, further increasing the time interval and making recall even more infrequent.

Infrequent products also result in a lack of habit formation. Without habit formation, every product-linked decision automatically carries a higher cognitive load. This in turn deters repeat purchases and can easily get channeled away by targeted advertising by other brands that offer a user-friendly, convenient, easy path to purchase. Brand loyalty is built through habit formation and frequent, predictable interactions over time. Lack of habit formation also implies repeated decision-making, which invariably leads to higher cognitive load and decision fatigue. This results in procrastination, delays, and lack of interest or engagement.

By tweaking their offering and building a data-driven portfolio of new digital assets, legacy businesses with infrequent products can also optimize mechanisms to grow. Viveck Kumar, product executive and former VP of product at PropertyGuru – Southeast Asia's largest real estate technology company – developed the ICED framework for businesses with infrequent products.[81] He focuses on the following four key dimensions of infrequent products:

1. **Infrequency**

   – Problem: Customers forget the product and brand between uses.

   – Solution: Build recall mechanisms like community features, regular updates, reminders, etc, and focus on creating

high-impact interactions every time the
product is used.

2. **Control**

   - Problem: Limited influence over the user's
     end-to-end experience and value delivery
     mechanism.

   - Solution: Increase control by owning more of
     the user journey and simplifying the process,
     to build trust and loyalty through convenience,
     ease of use, and data-driven personalization.

3. **Engagement**

   - Problem: Low engagement due to complexity,
     lack of frequent touchpoints, and unpredictable
     retention of rarely used legacy products.

   - Solution: Make interactions simple,
     provide constant touchpoints (eg, updates,
     notifications), and improve predictability with
     clear value delivery.

4. **Distinctiveness**

   - Problem: Lack of a memorable value
     proposition leads to reliance on ads or search
     engines for growth.

   - Solution: Create a unique offering that builds
     strong brand recall and drives organic traffic.

Behind every infrequent product, there is a more frequent transaction and corresponding flow of payment,

or the strong signal of a purchase intent for a whole range of other products and services. Both of these elements can be leveraged to build a data-driven layer of value creation on top of the infrequent legacy product. In the final section of this chapter, let's look at a systematic and iterative approach to building a highly leveraged, aligned, simplified, and optimized growth engine for any legacy business – even one that offers only infrequent products.

Connecting actions to outcomes

Inspired by Maslow's hierarchy of needs, I use the following pyramid to categorize high level the hierarchy and importance of the value-add created for customers.

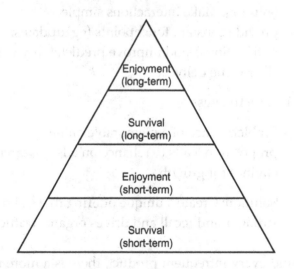

Hierarchy of needs (adapted from Maslow's Hierarchy)[82]

A tactical template to drive growth

1. Value-add can be content, research, intellectual property, digital products, community platforms, physical products, live online events, live in-person experiences, and more.

2. Start by leveraging your legacy business assets to build as much of the value-add as possible yourself.

3. Offer something value-add at all levels of the pyramid and do not restrict yourself to what you can currently produce or supply.

4. Especially for infrequent products, insert value-add onto existing transactions and payments. Otherwise, leverage a clear purchase intent for other products and services linked to the infrequent product you have sold by monetizing it, by offering additional products yourself or through relevant advertising for third-party products.

5. Take the remaining value-added opportunities that don't leverage your legacy business assets, and build partnerships to supply the best possible value-add with a high degree of control to drive engagement and increase the frequency of use.

6. Measure, model, experiment, and iterate to drive word-of-mouth recommendations and referrals,

to leverage network effects and positive feedback loops for virality.

Steps to help you to build your progressive impact funnel

1. Plot the retention curve to map and correlate actions to the changes in outcome along the user journey.

2. Optimize the placement of value-add along the funnel.

3. A good starting point is to distribute value-add from free at the start of the funnel to expensive at the end of the funnel.

4. Low switching costs at the start of the funnel to high switching costs at the end of the funnel.

5. The overall distribution of value-add along the funnel should build trust by educating your potential customers and market.

Guide for building your long-term optimized flywheel

1. Define your North Star metric inspired by the most common needs:

   – Price

   – Range

– Speed

– Convenience

2. Leverage legacy assets for data-driven value creation:

– Existing customer demand

– Data generated from physical assets, counter-positioning, etc

3. Simplify neutral tasks through data-driven algorithms and decision-making, and avoid investing in overhead.

4. Optimize the long-term flywheel to grow by considering:

– The entire distribution of outcomes to structure leveraged asymmetric bets

– Accelerate time to first value and the frequency of value delivery to drive engagement, habit formation, and retention by staying well above the nuisance threshold

– Simplify and standardize regularly to remove friction, avoid the growing costs of complexity, and prevent collapse

5. Recognize growth as a portfolio of iterative leveraged asymmetric bets with explore and

exploit loops, where you double down on what works:

- If successful, will this have the biggest impact possible?

- If it fails, what can be done in advance to reduce losses?

- Fail conclusively, and try to fail fast to minimize opportunity costs.

6. Obsess about what it would take for your customers to recommend your product by word of mouth.

DISCUSSION POINT: Grow in a world of demand and abundance

Discuss these five questions with your team so you can grow your business right away:

1. How can you shift from a scarcity mindset focused on resource constraints to an abundance mindset by prioritizing customer demand and unmet needs, and by leveraging data-driven technologies to deliver 10× better outcomes?

2. How can you look beyond your existing supply and unlock abundant demand to drive growth through targeted investments and partnerships?

3. How can you build your data-driven progressive impact funnel and long-term optimized flywheel to compound growth?

4. How can you solve for infrequent products by building a portfolio of higher-frequency

---

value-delivering data-driven products, content, and assets?

5. How can you leverage your legacy assets, align everything to a North Star metric, simplify the rest, and optimize by accelerating value delivery – while iterating with asymmetric bets, and focusing on word-of-mouth recommendations to grow?

Growth and profitability engines

The first of the two case studies below illustrates how a legacy business that is almost a century old built a highly leveraged, aligned, simplified, and optimized growth engine based on its legacy brand and assets. The second shows how a fifteen-year-old business successfully scaled in a legacy sector by offering a significantly superior, simplified, and customer-aligned leveraged product suite to drive phenomenal growth, primarily through word of mouth.

CASE STUDY: Building an optimized growth engine – How Bajaj Finance revolutionized consumer credit in India

Bajaj Finance, part of the family-owned Bajaj Group, has emerged as one of India's most dynamic non-banking financial companies (NBFCs). Banks offer comprehensive financial services, including deposit-taking, lending, payment services, investment products, and more. In contrast, NBFCs in India primarily deal in lending and investment activities, offering services like loans, asset financing, and investment advisory. By embracing the principles of disruptive innovation, excellence alongside scale, and long-term sustainable profitability, Bajaj Finance has built a data-driven growth machine. Between 2010 and 2023 the company expanded its loan book by compounding at 40% annually while achieving a compound annual growth rate (CAGR) of 25% in profit.[83] This case study examines how Bajaj Finance's strategic clarity, customer-centric obsession, and data-driven algorithms have put it in a league of its own in the very competitive financial services landscape of India.

Summary

Bajaj Finance was founded in 1987 as a captive finance company to support the purchase of Bajaj motorbikes and scooters. By the mid-2000s India's burgeoning middle class, and its rising consumer needs and aspirations, created new opportunities in consumer financing. However, the financial sector faced massive challenges like high credit risk, fragmented markets, and limited digital penetration.

Under the leadership of entrepreneur and owner Sanjiv Bajaj and CEO Rajeev Jain, Bajaj Finance evolved into a diversified NBFC with offerings spanning consumer, SME, commercial, and rural lending. The adoption of advanced data-driven algorithms and digital solutions allowed the company to target untapped customer segments while minimizing credit risk. By 2015 Bajaj Finance had grown into a multiproduct offering, leveraging its unique legacy asset of the Bajaj Group's trusted brand to scale rapidly while maintaining customer trust.

Challenges

The financial services industry in India is riddled with obstacles:

- **Brutal competition:** Banks and NBFCs were competing fiercely for market share, especially in the retail and SME customer segments.

- **High credit risk:** India's diverse demographic and economic disparities make it very challenging to maintain low NPAs (non-performing assets) across different types of lending.

- **Regulatory pressures:** Compliance requirements for NBFCs became increasingly stringent after the 2008 financial crisis, raising the cost of doing business and putting pressure on profit margins.

Bajaj Finance leveraged its legacy assets, aligned its business to the new aspirational middle class, simplified its user journey and processes, and optimized its growth engine to overcome these industry-wide challenges in the emerging market of India.

Methodology

Bajaj Finance adopted a multipronged approach to dominate the market:

1. **Leadership and vision**
   - Owner and entrepreneur Sanjiv Bajaj championed a culture of innovation while maintaining the Bajaj Group's legacy of trust and customer-centricity.
   - CEO Rajeev Jain drove the leveraged growth through strategic investments in technology and talent, scaling the company while generating healthy profits.

2. **Optimizing the product portfolio**

   – **Product diversification:** Bajaj Finance moved beyond vehicle financing to offer personal loans, credit cards, SME loans, and co-branded EMI cards.[84]

   – **Partnerships:** Extensive partnerships with consumer durables brands were established to provide customers with the most competitive offers.

   – **Consumer ecosystem:** The self-service "Bajaj Finserv App" was created to provide end-to-end financial services, from loan applications to insurance purchases, introducing a product-led growth motion.[85]

3. **Excellence alongside scale**

   – **Technology investments:** Data-driven algorithms were implemented for credit scoring, enabling faster, streamlined, and more robust underwriting and better risk assessment.

   – **Data-driven decisions:** A suite of centralized, data-driven models was built to analyze customer behavior and predict future needs, leading to personalized loan offerings.

   – **Operational efficiency:** Back-office processes were digitized to reduce turnaround times for loan approvals from several days to just a few minutes.

4. **Long-term sustainable profitability**

   – **Risk management:** Granular risk profiling was used to maintain NPAs at often around just 1% – significantly lower than the industry average.[86]

- **Customer engagement:** Focus was placed on cross-selling financial products to existing customers, through loyalty programs and targeted campaigns, to drive frequency of transactions, customer engagement, and brand recall.
- **Branch-lite profitable model:** Overhead costs were reduced by combining physical presence in key markets with a strong digital footprint.

Outcomes

Bajaj Finance achieved exceptional results, solidifying its position as a market leader, through:

- **Financial growth**
  - Assets under management grew from about USD 120 million in 2006 to more than USD 42 billion by 2025.
  - Customer numbers grew from about 2 million customers in 2010 to more than 88 million in 2025.
  - Portfolio synergies: Active, data-driven cross-selling resulted in 70% of all customers buying at least two products.
- **Operational excellence**
  - Loan approval times of under ten minutes were achieved for digital applications.
  - More than 40% of users are self-serve, using the digital app and platform.[87]
  - Profit after tax has a sixteen-year CAGR of a whopping 52%.[88]

- **Market leadership**
  - Bajaj Finance has become India's largest NBFC by market capitalization, surpassing all other traditional competitors.
  - The company has dominated the EMI financing space, with 70% market share in consumer durable loans through financed sales in more than 91,000 consumer retail stores in India.[89]

Key takeaways

1. **Data is a leveraged asset:** Bajaj Finance's use of data-driven algorithms and real-time data-driven decision-making allowed for hyper-personalization and rigorous credit risk assessment.

2. **Impact requires aligned leadership:** Sanjiv Bajaj and Rajeev Jain's alignment on long-term goals and values was crucial to driving double-digit, rapid, compounded growth over more than a decade.

3. **Customer-centric simplicity wins:** By prioritizing simplicity, accessibility, and affordability, Bajaj Finance created a loyal customer base that swears by the brand.

4. **Optimize technology for growth:** The company's emphasis on technology focused on growth ensured it scaled efficiently without compromising profit margins.

Conclusion

Bajaj Finance's evolution into a fast-growing, data-driven financial powerhouse is a testament to its winning approach. By leveraging its legacy assets in a digital data-driven manner and aligning everyone to customer impact, along with simplifying the customer experience and processes, Bajaj Finance built an optimized growth machine that outperformed traditional NBFCs and banks in India.

As Bajaj Finance continues to expand into new verticals like wealth management and payments, its resounding category-defining success offers a blueprint for companies seeking to win in legacy industries with sustainable, scalable, and profitable growth.

CASE STUDY: Revolutionizing currency transfers – How Wise built a global growth engine

How far would you go to delight your customers? When Wise (formerly TransferWise) found out that its customers wanted ever faster payments, it thought from first principles to find out how it could fulfill this customer wish. There were many ways to speed up the transfers by a little bit, and even by combining those approaches, the outcome wouldn't be orders of magnitude faster. The holy grail was to enable instant transfer – that didn't yet exist, and it would blow the customers' minds. The only way to achieve instant payments was to plug directly into central banks. Wise spent three to four years lobbying the government to create a sandbox environment, through which ambitious FinTechs could plug directly into the Bank of England. It then took another four to five years to build this out. Delighting customers by building things that don't exist is hard, but it is also one of the few ways of compounding growth profitably.

Summary

Wise disrupted the global financial landscape by addressing inefficiencies in currency exchange and international money transfers. Founded in 2011 by

Kristo Käärmann and Taavet Hinrikus, the company leveraged transparency, technology, and customer-centric solutions to create a platform that undercut traditional banks on cost and convenience. By 2023 Wise had more than 16 million customers and transferred more than £120 billion annually, saving users billions in hidden fees. This case study explores how the leadership of the founders Kristo Käärmann and Taavet Hinrikus, as well as Chief Product Officer Nilan Peiris and others, optimized growth through:

- Leveraging transparency of value delivered to customers
- Alignment to the core needs of price, speed, and convenience of customers
- Data-driven optimization of decision-making
- Relentless focus on growth through customer recommendation and advocacy[90]

Context

Before Wise was born, sending money across borders was expensive, opaque, cumbersome, and inefficient. Traditional banks, benefiting from a lack of transparency in international transfers, charged high fees and offered poor exchange rates, resulting in total costs of more than 5%. Kristo Käärmann and Taavet Hinrikus, Estonian expatriates in London, experienced these frustrations firsthand. Hinrikus needed pounds, while Käärmann needed euros. By exchanging funds directly peer to peer, they realized significant savings, laying the foundation for Wise.

Founded in 2011, Wise entered a space dominated by entrenched financial institutions. Early challenges included building trust, achieving scale, and navigating stringent regulatory requirements in multiple jurisdictions in a legacy industry.

Challenges

Wise faced several challenges in its early growth journey:

- **Uninformed customers:** Consumers were accustomed to tolerating intransparent legacy banks, despite high fees, and lacked awareness of cheaper alternatives.
- **Regulatory hurdles:** Operating in the heavily regulated legacy financial sector requires compliance with diverse laws across countries.
- **Global scaling:** Building a seamless platform for multicurrency transfers required advanced infrastructure and partnerships with banks globally, including working closely with central banks.

Methodology

Wise addressed these challenges with a multifaceted approach:

1. **Leadership and radical transparency**
   - Hidden fees in traditional bank transfers were highlighted, educating customers about real costs.
   - Mid-market exchange rates were prominently displayed, ensuring users knew exactly what fees they were paying.

2. **Customer-centric product development**
   - Focus was placed on fast transfer times, by improving the status quo 10×, lowering transfer times from three to five days to at most two

days. By plugging directly into central banks, in some cases transfer times were reduced to instant payments.[91]

- Ultra-low transfer fees were prioritized by improving the status quo 10×, lowering transfer costs by an order of magnitude compared with alternatives.

3. **Growth and marketing strategy**

- Nilan Peiris spearheaded data-driven customer evangelism, recommendation, and word of mouth to drive profitable growth.[92]

- Wise invested in creative, localized marketing campaigns that resonated with diverse audiences and shared Wise's Mission "Money without borders: instant, convenient, transparent, and eventually free," with customers to galvanize them.

Outcomes

Wise's approach yielded exceptional results:

- **Customer growth:** More than 16 million customers globally were gained by 2023, with strong retention and acquisition metrics.

- **Market share:** More than £120 billion was transferred annually across 80+ countries, making Wise a leader in international money transfers.[93]

- **Cost savings:** Customers saved an estimated £1.5 billion annually compared with traditional banks, solidifying Wise's value proposition.

- **Revenue and profitability:** Wise achieved profitability early in its journey from 2017 and maintained consistent growth, reporting just over £1 billion in revenue for the twelve months from March 2023 to March 2024.[94]

Key takeaways

1. **Transparency builds trust:** Wise's commitment to honesty and clarity created strong customer loyalty, setting it apart in a traditionally opaque industry.

2. **Customer-centricity drives growth:** User-focused innovations like multicurrency accounts and referral incentives directly addressed pain points, fueling organic growth.

3. **Localized scaling is critical:** Working closely with central banks, and compliance with regional regulations, allowed for scaling across more than seventy markets globally.

4. **Leadership and culture matter:** A mission-driven culture and visionary leadership from Peiris, Käärmann, and Hinrikus set a high bar for performance. Nilan Peiris ran regular "Walk the Product" sessions every two weeks with teams – not for assessing new products, but for core, frequently used features and user flows. This led to relentless improvements and optimization of the core value proposition of Wise's mission and promise to its customers.

Conclusion

Wise revolutionized currency transfers by combining transparency, technology, and growth, all driven by customer evangelism, advocacy, and recommendation. The leadership of founders Kristo Käärmann, Taavet Hinrikus, and Chief Product Officer Nilan Peiris was instrumental in building a global growth engine that challenged traditional banks and set new standards for the industry.

As Wise continues to expand into new markets and services, its story offers valuable and actionable insights for businesses aiming to disrupt legacy industries. By leveraging efficiency, building customer trust through transparency and technology, and aligning its mission with value delivered to customers, Wise not only revolutionized currency transfers but also demonstrated the power of purpose-driven, customer-led evangelism and profitable growth.

Conclusion: Take Back Control Of Your Destiny

In school my English teacher used to call me "Bonsai Master." While my classmates wrote long essays, I struggled to write more than a page or so. I would condense all my ideas into a few paragraphs and stop. In contrast, I wrote this book of more than 35,000 words in six weeks. When you have clarity and the courage to act, impact is an inevitability.

Your customers are evolving at the fastest rate ever. More than half of all romantic relationships now are through people being matched by a dating algorithm. During the next decade or so, more than half of newborns will be e-babies, born to parents who met via algorithms. Even before their birth, your customers have been conceived via a data-driven algorithm, instead of a historical, evolutionary mechanism.

As you read this, a new generation of customers entering your market has grown up in this world, and this new generation knows nothing but on-demand access and personalization. For the first time in human history, your new customers have been shaped from birth by nature, nurture, and algorithms. From an evolutionary perspective, they're now wired differently. You need to act now.

Defining intelligence is somewhat of a wicked problem, but the following evolutionary definition tries to distill the essence of intelligence to its most generalized yet actionable form: intelligence is the ability to adapt to new paradigms, to thrive and grow. You need to be a data company that just happens to own a legacy business.

Let's summarize the benefits of the SLASOG Framework:

1. **Save:** Most legacy businesses struggle to adapt to the data-driven paradigm by wasting enormous resources on spraying and praying and boiling the ocean, which is guaranteed to fail. You are now equipped to save money right from the outset. You can then invest that capital to win in the data-driven paradigm.

2. **Leverage:** Most companies settle for consensus-based, politically safe sevens and engage in probability matching instead of focusing on the highest-impact opportunities.

You now know how to leverage your customer demand and your unfair non-digital advantage as well as counter-positioning.

3. **Align:** Most companies struggle to execute, frittering away resources without being able to focus impact on the bullseye. You know now how to align your entire business to value delivery for your customers, and to marshal a data-driven, combined-arms approach to align everything to your leveraged opportunities.

4. **Simplify:** Most companies put digital band-aids on legacy processes, resulting in inferior experiences for customers, crippling costs of complexity, and risk of collapse. Now you know how to rethink and reengineer processes to simplify and boost the returns of your leveraged and aligned approach.

5. **Optimize:** Most companies operate with a sub-optimal decision-making framework that either glosses over uncertainty, randomizes, or oversimplifies in the wrong way. You now know how to build an empirically valid and mathematically optimizable model of the world to allow you to maximize your wins.

6. **Grow:** Most legacy businesses are constrained by a scarcity mindset based on costs and available resources. You have now embraced abundance and know how to build your data-driven funnel and flywheel so that you can leverage, align,

simplify, and optimize your growth model to achieve maximum returns.

The case studies in this book have illustrated how a wide range of varied legacy businesses have adopted vastly different but always successful playbooks, empowering them to adapt and thrive in the digital, data-driven paradigm.

On www.slasog.com I invite you to join a thriving data impact-obsessed community to find a universe of new and updated resources, to empower you to apply SLASOG to your business.

You are now equipped with all the actionable insights and playbooks to SLASOG your business. Give your team a copy of this book, and start building a data-driven company.

First, though, sit back and do a Gedankenexperiment of what it feels like to win.

Notes

1 P Saffo, "Forecasting is 'Strong Opinions, Weakly Held'"
   (SKMurphy), www.skmurphy.com/blog/2010/08/16/
   paul-saffo-forecasting-is-strong-opinions-weakly-held,
   accessed January 29, 2025 (reproduced with permission
   from Paul Saffo)
2 R Federer, "2024 Commencement Address by
   Roger Federer at Dartmouth," www.youtube.com/
   watch?v=pqWUuYTcG-o, accessed January 20, 2025
3 Amazon Web Services, "2012 re:Invent Day 2: Fireside Chat
   with Jeff Bezos & Werner Vogels," www.youtube.com/
   watch?v=O4MtQGRIIuA, accessed January 28, 2025
4 L-P Baculard et al., *Orchestrating a Successful Digital
   Transformation* (Bain & Company, 2017), www.bain.com/
   contentassets/dd440ca288d34c16ba8cd3ab6ef69a04/bain_
   brief_orchestrating_a_successful_digital_transformation.
   pdf, accessed January 21, 2025
5 M Wade and J Shan, "Covid-19 Has Accelerated Digital
   Transformation, but May Have Made it Harder Not
   Easier," *MIS Quarterly Executive*, 19/3 (2020), https://doi.
   org/10.17705/2msqe.00034

6 M Lerner, "Sevens Kill Companies" (SYSTM, March 1, 2022), www.systm.co/post/sevens-kill-companies, accessed February 5, 2025

7 KK Ladha, "Information pooling through majority-rule voting: Condorcet's jury theorem with correlated votes," *Journal of Economic Behavior & Organization*, 26/3 (May 1995), 353–372, https://doi.org/10.1016/0167-2681(94)00068-P

8 C Munger, "A Lesson on Elementary Worldly Wisdom As It Relates To Investment Management & Business" [transcript], (Farnam Street Media Inc.), https://fs.blog/great-talks/a-lesson-on-worldly-wisdom, accessed January 29, 2025

9 HWJ Rittel and MM Webber, "Dilemmas in a general theory of planning," *Policy Sciences*, 4/2 (1973), 155–169, https://doi.org/10.1007/BF01405730

10 J Conklin, *Dialogue Mapping: Building shared understanding of wicked problems* (Wiley, 2005)

11 C Munger, "Show me the incentive, I'll show you the outcome" (Schroders, May 3, 2017), www.schroders.com/en-au/au/adviser/insights/show-me-the-incentive-ill-show-you-the-outcome, accessed February 5, 2025

12 GRF Brown, *The Napoleonic Wars and United States Marine Corps Warfighting Functions* (United States Marine Corps, 2002), https://apps.dtic.mil/sti/tr/pdf/ADA401266.pdf, accessed February 5, 2025

13 B Jacobs, "Billionaire Brad Jacobs: Meditation, thought experiments, and cognitive behavior therapy helped me succeed—and can do the same for you" (yahoo!finance, April 4, 2024), https://finance.yahoo.com/news/billionaire-brad-jacobs-meditation-thought-142833729.html, accessed January 21, 2025

14 A Narayanan and S Kapoor, *AI Snake Oil: What artificial intelligence can do, what it can't, and how to tell the difference* (Princeton University Press, 2024)

15 TJ Brennan and AW Lo, "An Evolutionary Model of Bounded Rationality and Intelligence," *PLoS One*, 7/11, (2012), doi: 10.1371/journal.pone.0050310

16 HA Simon, *Rational Decision-Making in Business Organizations*, Nobel Memorial Lecture, Carnegie-Mellon University, Pittsburgh (December 8, 1978), www.nobelprize.org/uploads/2018/06/simon-lecture.pdf, accessed January 22, 2025

17 EW Dijkstra, "The humble programmer" (ACM Turing Award Lectures, 1972), https://doi. org/10.1145/1283920.1283927

18 PF Drucker, *The Practice of Management* (HarperCollins Publishers, 1954)

19 G Sitaraman, "Airlines Are Just Banks Now," The Atlantic (September 21, 2023), www.theatlantic.com/ ideas/archive/2023/09/airlines-banks-mileage-programs/675374, accessed January 29, 2025

20 ProjectPro, "How Big Data Analysis helped increase Walmarts Sales turnover?" (ProjectPro, October 11, 2024), www.projectpro.io/article/how-big-data-analysis-helped-increase-walmarts-sales-turnover/109, accessed January 22, 2025

21 M Reustle and S Mukherjea, "Bajaj Finance: Strategies of a Lending Giant," Business Breakdowns podcast, episode 165, (2024), www.youtube.com/watch?v=608pEFUBL80, accessed February 5, 2025

22 D Kulak, "The Business Strategy Silicon Valley Giants Use to Disrupt Industries" (LeadingAgile), www.leadingagile. com/2021/03/heres-the-business-strategy-silicon-valley-giants-use-to-disrupt-industries-you-can-use-it-for-your-business, accessed February 2, 2025

23 J Piela, "Gespräche zur digitalen Transformation in der Versicherungswirtschaft" (piela&co), https://pielaco.com/ podcast/episodes-huk24, accessed January 23, 2025

24 EG Saunders, "How to Allocate Your Time, and Your Effort," *Harvard Business Review* (January 7, 2013), https:// hbr.org/2013/01/how-to-allocate-your-time-and, accessed January 29, 2025

25 S Doshi, (@shreyas), "Introducing the LNO Effectiveness Framework" (February 2, 2020), https://x.com/shreyas/ status/1223816226918453253, accessed January 29, 2025

26 Used with permission, S Doshi, (@shreyas), "A thread of product management frameworks" (May 30, 2021), https://x.com/shreyas/status/1399061782560350208, accessed February 27, 2025

27 Used with permission, S Doshi, (@shreyas), "A thread of product management frameworks"

28 WH McRaven, *The Theory of Special Operations* (master's thesis, Naval Postgraduate School Monterey, June 17, 1993), www.afsoc.af.mil/Portals/86/documents/history/AFD-051228-021.pdf, accessed January 23, 2025

29 J Piela, "Was sich aus der Geschichte der HUK24 zum Aufbau eines Online-Versicherers lernen lässt" (piela&co), https://pielaco.com/podcast/episodes/der-aufbau-eines-direktversicherers-mit-detlef-frank-und-uwe-stuhldreier, accessed January 23, 2025

30 J Mirzadegan, "Episode 140: CRO Walmart, Seth Dallaire – How You Show Up," Grit (May 29, 2023), https://open.spotify.com/episode/6V5PDdcZ7v3QNXxzA3q3Mc, accessed January 23, 2025

31 Romeo Man, "Sean Ellis On The Backbone Of Successful Growth Teams & The North Star Metric", StartUs Magazine (29 January 2020), https://magazine.startus.cc/sean-ellis-on-the-backbone-of-successful-growth-teams-the-north-star-metric, accessed 11 March 2025

32 M Lerner, *Growth Levers and How to Find Them* (SYSTM, 2023)

33 C Zook, "Commander's Intent" (Thinkers 50), https://thinkers50.com/blog/commanders-intent, accessed January 29, 2025

34 US Marine Corps University, "8-2 Importance, CoA War Game," www.usmcu.edu/Portals/218/MCPP/8908%20IMI%20Module%208/8908%20IMI%20Module%208/2/index.html, accessed January 30, 2025

35 E Gil, "An interview with Claire Hughes Johnson," *High Growth Handbook*, https://growth.eladgil.com/book/the-role-of-the-ceo/decision-making-and-managing-executives-an-interview-with-claire-hughes-johnson, accessed January 29, 2025

36 C Blair, *Hitler's U-Boat War: The hunters, 1939–1942* (Random House USA, 1996); SE Morison, *Battle of the Atlantic 1939–1945* (Castle Books, 2001); D Syrett, *The Defeat of the German U-boats: Battle of the Atlantic* (University of South Carolina Press, 1994); uboat.net, "U-boat Fates," www.uboat.net/fates/losses, accessed February 5, 2025

37 S Bahcall, *Loonshots: How to nurture the crazy ideas that win wars, cure diseases, and transform industries* (St Martin's Press, 2019)

38 M Goodall, "Building Better Business: Interview with Greg Jackson, Founder of Octopus" (Guild, May 24, 2023), https://guild.co/blog/building-better-business-interview-greg-jackson-octopus, accessed January 29, 2025

39 Octopus Energy, "What it's like to work at Octopus"
    (Octopus Energy), https://octopusenergy.com/careers,
    accessed January 24, 2025
40 Octopus Energy, "Octopus Energy Group results for FY23,"
    https://octopus.energy/press/Octopus-Energy-Group-
    results-for-FY23, accessed January 29, 2025
41 Z Fuss, "Roper Technologies: Industrial Titan to
    Software Giant," Business Breakdowns podcast,
    episode 108 (2023), https://open.spotify.com/
    episode/11D8NTXGRgIfIzdyogloC2, accessed January 29,
    2025
42 Roper Technologies, "Roper Technologies announces 2023
    financial results" (Roper Technologies, January 31, 2024),
    www.ropertech.com/news-releases/news-release-details/
    roper-technologies-announces-2023-financial-results,
    accessed January 29, 2025
43 Business Observer, "Area executive, a Wall Street rock
    star, dies at 73," Business Observer (November 5, 2018),
    www.businessobserverfl.com/news/2018/nov/05/
    area-executive-a-wall-street-rock-star-dies-at-73, accessed
    January 29, 2025
44 J Bronchick, "The Industrial World Just Lost a Great
    Leader" (Cove Street Capital), https://covestreetcapital.
    com/the-industrial-world-just-lost-a-great-leader, accessed
    January 29, 2025
45 Roper Technologies, "Proxy Statement" (Roper
    Technologies, April 30, 2018), www.sec.gov/Archives/
    edgar/data/882835/000119312518143597/d465849ddef14a.
    htm, accessed January 29, 2025
46 A Saint-Exupéry, Airman's Odyssey (Mariner Books, 1984)
47 N Eyal, Hooked: How to build habit-forming products (Portfolio
    Penguin, 2014)
48 Used with permission and adapted from N Eyal, "The
    Hooked Model: How to Manufacture Desire in 4 Steps"
    (Nir and Far, no date), www.nirandfar.com/how-to-
    manufacture-desire, accessed February 27, 2025
49 L Rachitsky, "Behind the product: Duolingo streaks," Lenny's
    Podcast (2024), www.lennysnewsletter.com/p/behind-the-
    product-duolingo-streaks, accessed January 29, 2025
50 Used with permission, S Doshi, (@shreyas), "A thread
    of product management frameworks" (May 30, 2021),
    https://x.com/shreyas/status/1399061782560350208,
    accessed February 27, 2025

51 J Champy and M Hammer, *Reengineering the Corporation: A manifesto for business revolution* (Nicholas Brealey Publishing, 1993)

52 JA Tainter, *The Collapse of Complex Societies* (Cambridge University Press, 1988)

53 A Saxenian, *Regional Advantage: Culture and competition in Silicon Valley and Route 128* (Harvard University Press, 1996)

54 P Raj, "Competition & Strategy" (Prateek Raj), www. prateekr.com/strategy-notes.html, accessed January 29, 2025

55 B Manning, "How Silicon Valley Became Silicon Valley (And Why Boston Came In Second)" (Brian Manning, April 7, 2019), www.briancmanning.com/blog/2019/4/7/how-silicon-valley-became-silicon-valley, accessed January 29, 2025

56 A Gupta and H Wang, "The Reason Silicon Valley Beat Out Boston for VC Dominance," *Harvard Business Review* (November 15, 2016), https://hbr.org/2016/11/the-reason-silicon-valley-beat-out-boston-for-vc-dominance, accessed January 29, 2025

57 OMR, "Ronald Slabke: Der Milliardär, der zur Miete wohnt," OMR Podcast #420 (2021), www.youtube.com/watch?v=y7zBqCN-Fpk, accessed January 28, 2025

58 Hypoport, *Hypoport SE Annual Report for 2022* (Hypoport, March 27, 2023), www.hypoport.com/wp-content/uploads/2023/03/Annual_Report_Hypoport_2022-1.pdf, accessed January 29, 2025

59 Hypoport, *Hypoport SE Annual Report for 2022*

60 B Jacobs, *How to Make a Few Billion Dollars* (Greenleaf Book Group LLC, 2024)

61 B Jacobs, *How to Make a Few Billion Dollars*

62 XPO, "XPO Logistics Ranked as the Largest Logistics Company in North America" (XPO, April 5, 2017), https://news.xpo.com/506/xpo-logistics-ranked-as-the-largest-logistics-company-in-north-america, accessed January 29, 2025

63 XPO, "XPO Logistics to Acquire Con-way" [press release] (XPO, September 9, 2015), https://investors.xpo.com/news-releases/news-release-details/xpo-logistics-acquire-con-way, accessed January 29, 2025

64 XPO, "XPO Logistics to Acquire Norbert Dentressangle SA" (XPO, April 28, 2015), https://news.xpo.com/563/

xpo-logistics-to-acquire-norbert-dentressangle-sa-a-
leading-global-provider-of-, accessed January 29, 2025

65 XPO, "XPO Announces Fourth Quarter and Full Year 2022
Results" [press release] (XPO, February 8, 2023), www.
xpo.com/cdn/files/s24/XPOQ42022_EarningsPress_
ReleaseVF85.pdf, accessed January 29, 2025

66 GXO, "GXO Logistics, Inc. Completes Spin-Off from
XPO Logistics, Inc." [press release] (GXO, August 2,
2021), https://gxo.com/news_article/gxo-logistics-inc-
completes-spin-off-from-xpo-logistics-inc, accessed January
29, 2025

67 B Jacobs, *How to Make a Few Billion Dollars*

68 The Cynefin Company, "The Cynefin Framework,"
https://thecynefin.co/about-us/about-cynefin-framework,
accessed January 29, 2025

69 B George, "Why Boeing's Problems with the 737 MAX
Began More Than 25 Years Ago," (Harvard Business
School, January 24, 2024), www.library.hbs.edu/working-
knowledge/why-boeings-problems-with-737-max-began-
more-than-25-years-ago, accessed February 5, 2025

70 Institute of Business Forecasting & Planning, "What
Is Forecast Value Added (FVA)?," https://ibf.org/
knowledge/glossary/forecast-value-added-fva-131,
accessed January 29, 2025

71 Lokad, "Initiative of Quantitative Supply Chain," www.
lokad.com/introduction-to-quantitative-supply-chain,
accessed January 29, 2025

72 Lokad, "Optimizing Omnichannel Retail at Worten"
(LinkedIn, February 4, 2025), www.linkedin.com/posts/
lokad_optimizing-omnichannel-retail-at-worten-activity-
7292177956360122368-CYwq, accessed February 5, 2025

73 T Dotan, "Here's a look inside Instacart's playbook to
take on Google and Facebook as it tries to build a USD
1 billion ads business," *Business Insider* (June 14, 2021),
www.businessinsider.com/instacart-advertising-business-
revenue-ipo-amazon-seth-dallaire-2021-6, accessed January
29, 2025

74 T Dotan, "Here's a look inside Instacart's playbook to take
on Google and Facebook as it tries to build a USD 1 billion
ads business"

75 Christensen Institute, "Disruptive Innovation Theory,"
(Christensen Institute), www.christenseninstitute.org/
theory/disruptive-innovation, accessed January 29, 2025

76 J Dalton and A Logan, "Lessons from the Rise of Netflix
    and the Fall of Blockbuster" (Cato Institute, October 26,
    2024), www.cato.org/commentary/lessons-rise-netflix-fall-
    blockbuster, accessed February 5, 2025; KA Grant, "How
    Netflix Slowly Disrupted the Movie Rental Industry &
    Paved the Way for Today's Streaming Services" (KA Grant,
    April 12, 2022), https://kagrant.com/the-netflix-way,
    accessed February 5, 2025

77 CM Christensen et al., "What Is Disruptive Innovation?,"
    Harvard Business Review (December 2015), https://hbr.
    org/2015/12/what-is-disruptive-innovation, accessed
    January 25, 2025

78 S Mullainathan and E Shafir, *Scarcity: Why having too little
    means so much* (Allen Lane, 2013)

79 SP Choudary, "Amazon is a logistics beast – A detailed
    teardown" (Substack, May 13, 2020), https://platforms.
    substack.com/p/amazon-is-a-logistics-beast-a-detailed,
    accessed January 26, 2025

80 RL Davis and Y Zhong, "The Biology of Forgetting—A
    Perspective," *Neuron*, 95/3 (2017), 490–503, https://doi.
    org/10.1016/j.neuron.2017.05.039

81 V Kumar, "Manage infrequent products with ICED theory"
    (Reforge), www.reforge.com/guides/manage-infrequent-
    products-with-iced-theory, accessed January 29, 2025

82 AH Maslow, (1943). "A Theory Of Human Motivation,"
    Psychological Review, 50/4 (1943), 370–396, https://doi.
    org/10.1037/h0054346

83 M Reustle and S Mukherjea, "Bajaj Finance: Strategies
    of a Lending Giant," Business Breakdowns podcast,
    episode 165

84 S Mallick, "Bajaj Finance joins hands with Airtel to offer
    financial products – Loans, EMI card and more (ET Now,
    January 21, 2025), www.etnownews.com/companies/bajaj-
    finance-joins-hands-with-airtel-to-financial-products-loans-
    emi-card-and-more-article-117401173, accessed 5 February
    5, 2025

85 Bajaj Finance, *Bajaj Finance at a Glance* (Bajaj Finance, 2022),
    www.bajajfinserv.in/finance-digital-annual-report-fy22/
    finance-digital-annual-report-assets/pdf/BFL-Bajaj-
    Finance-at-a-Glance.pdf, accessed January 29, 2025

86 Money Control, "Bajaj Finance Q2 net profit rises 13%
    to Rs 4,000 crore, misses estimates," *MoneyControl*

News (October 22, 2024), www.moneycontrol.com/
europe/?url=https://www.moneycontrol.com/news/
business/earnings/bajaj-finance-q2-results-net-profit-rises-
13-to-rs-4000-cr-12848032.html, accessed January 30, 2025

87 Bajaj Finserv, "Personal Loan Approval Process and Time"
(Bajaj Finserv, May 25, 2021),www.bajajfinserv.in/insights/
personal-loan-approval-time, accessed January 30, 2025

88 Bajaj Finserv, *36th Annual Report, 2022–2023* (Bajaj Finance
Limited, 2023), www.bajajfinserv.in/finance-digital-annual-
report-fy23/financial-snapshot.html, accessed January 30,
2025

89 Marcellus, "Bajaj Finance: The Enigma Is Set For Another
Transformation" (Marcellus, July 17, 2021), https://
marcellus.in/newsletter/kings-of-capital/bajaj-finance-
the-enigma-is-set-for-another-transformation, accessed
January 30, 2025

90 N Peiris, "Nilan Peiris – 10 years Wiser: Lessons
learned from scaling Wise" (2024), www.youtube.com/
watch?v=oYcnWSW2eF8, accessed January 30, 2025

91 N Peiris, "Nilan Peiris – 10 years Wiser: Lessons learned
from scaling Wise"

92 N Peiris, "How to drive word of mouth," Lenny's Podcast
(2023), www.youtube.com/watch?v=xZifSLGOrrw,
accessed January 30, 2025

93 N Peiris, "Nilan Peiris – 10 years Wiser: Lessons learned
from scaling Wise"

94 Wise, *Wise 2024 Annual Report and Accounts* (Wise, 2024),
https://wise.com/imaginary-v2/images/3f1628373b21
2ca54c1ac73c68d69b72-WISE-2024-Annual-Report-and-
Accounts.pdf, accessed January 30, 2025

Further Reading

Save

Bezos, J, *Invent and Wander: The collected writings of Jeff Bezos* (Harvard Business Review Press, 2020)

Hastings R and Meyer E, *No Rules Rules: Netflix and the culture of reinvention* (Penguin Press, 2020)

Jacobs, B, *How to Make a Few Billion Dollars* (Greenleaf Book Group LLC, 2024)

Quartr, "Collection: Jeff Bezos Shareholder Letters" (Quartr, April 3, 2023), https://quartr.com/insights/business-philosophy/collection-jeff-bezos-shareholder-letters, accessed January 30, 2025

Stone, B, *Amazon Unbound: Jeff Bezos and the invention of a global empire* (Simon & Schuster, 2021)

Stone, B, *The Everything Store: Jeff Bezos and the age of Amazon* (Corgi, 2014)

Wade, M and Shan, J, "Covid-19 Has Accelerated Digital Transformation, but May Have Made it Harder Not Easier," *MIS Quarterly Executive*, 19/3 (2020), https://doi.org/10.17705/2msqe.00034

Leverage

Bitterman, ME et al., "Some Comparative Psychology of Learning," *New York Academy of Sciences* 69/3 (1958), 412–426

Brennan, TJ and Lo, AW, "An Evolutionary Model of Bounded Rationality and Intelligence," *PLoS One*, 7/11 (2012), https://doi: 10.1371/journal.pone.0050310

Herrnstein, RJ, "Relative and Absolute Strength of Response as a Function of Frequency of Reinforcement," *Journal of the Experimental Analysis of Behavior* 4/3 (1961), 267–272, https://doi.org/10.1901/jeab.1961.4-267

Lerner, M, *Growth Levers and How to Find Them* (SYSTM, 2023)

Mailleux, A-C et al., "How do ants assess food volume?" *Animal Behaviour*, 59/5 (2010), 1061–1069, https://doi.org/10.1006/anbe.2000.1396

McRaven, WH, *The Theory of Special Operations* (master's thesis, Naval Postgraduate School

Monterey, June 17, 1993), www.afsoc.af.mil/
Portals/86/documents/history/AFD-051228-021.
pdf, accessed January 23, 2025

Align

Bahcall, S, *Loonshots: How to nurture the crazy ideas that win wars, cure diseases, and transform industries* (St Martin's Press, 2019)

Simplify

Courtney, H et al., "Strategy Under Uncertainty," *Harvard Business Review* (November–December 1997), https://hbr.org/1997/11/strategy-under-uncertainty, accessed January 28, 2025

Eyal, N, *Hooked: How to build habit-forming products* (Portfolio Penguin, 2014)

Jacobs, B, *How to Make a Few Billion Dollars* (Greenleaf Book Group LLC, 2024)

Optimize

Mehrotra, S and Yamashita, Y, "Config 2024: Rituals to unbreak planning," www.youtube.com/watch?v=ltBlkap_AJI, accessed January 28, 2025

Mehrotra, S and Yamashita, Y, "Figma Config Talk: Rituals to Unbreak Planning" (Figma, 2024), https://coda.io/@shishir/figmaconfig2024, accessed January 28, 2025

Yang, P, "This Framework Will Change How You Think about Your Career" (Substack, September 8, 2024), https://creatoreconomy.so/p/the-best-framework-for-career-growth-shishir, accessed January 28, 2025

Grow

Christensen, CM et al., "What Is Disruptive Innovation?," *Harvard Business Review* (December 2015), https://hbr.org/2015/12/what-is-disruptive-innovation, accessed January 25, 2025

Croll, A and Yoskovitz, B, *Lean Analytics* (O'Reilly, 2013)

Kumar, V, "ICED Theory – Growing Infrequent Products," (Reforge), www.reforge.com/blog/iced-theory-growing-infrequent-products, accessed January 28, 2025

Kumar, V, "Un-BELT your consumer problems to create a successful infrequent products" (Substack, May 24, 2022), https://lowfrequencyproducts.substack.com/p/un-belt-your-consumer-problems-to, accessed January 28, 2025

Wessel, M and Christensen, CM, "Surviving Disruption?," *Harvard Business Review* (December 2012), https://hbr.org/2012/12/surviving-disruption, accessed January 28, 2025

Acknowledgments

I am grateful to all those who helped and supported the creation of this book:

- My wife and family
- Dr Marco Adelt
- Rethink Press team
- Mo Syed
- Dr Baptiste Goujaud
- Aurodeep Mukherjee
- Dr Uwe Stuhldreier
- Detlef Frank
- Shamik Biswas

- Joannès Vermorel and Lokad
- Conor Doherty
- Satya Sciavina
- Rahul Dharod
- Ankita Tapas
- Christoph Mayer
- Meera Chikermane
- Frederik Raspé
- Julian Werner
- Brian Hall
- Useful Book Community
- Rob Fitzpatrick
- Safi Bahcall
- Shreyas Doshi
- Viveck Kumar
- Paul Saffo
- Nir Eyal
- Daniel Priestley

The Author

Ritavan is an entrepreneurial technology leader with a decade of experience focused on data-driven business impact. He has authored peer-reviewed papers, given invited talks at global conferences, and holds an international patent. Known for his first principles approach to building and scaling data-driven solutions across industries, Ritavan combines deep technical expertise with strategic vision and an execution-focused mindset. His latest book offers actionable insights to accelerate data-driven value creation for legacy businesses.

🌐 www.ritavan.com